RA
A
EFFIC
REAI

RAPID AND EFFICIENT READING

COLIN MARES

EMERSON BOOKS, INC.
Buchanan, New York 10511

1977

PUBLISHED 1967 BY EMERSON BOOKS, INC.

Library of Congress Catalog Card Number: 67-29895

Second Printing, 1977

CONTENTS

INTRODUCTION

MOST people read at speeds and standards of efficiency which are far lower than those at which they are capable of reading with enjoyment and profit. This book is to help people who are aware that their reading abilities are inadequate and who wish to improve.

A great deal of sensational nonsense has been written about rapid reading speeds. Although parts of this book are concerned with the skills and techniques of rapid reading it must be made clear that rapid reading means rapid and accurate understanding. It is meaningless to talk of someone having "a reading speed of x words a minute". Speed cannot function in isolation. We read so that we may understand. Consequently, "reading speeds" can only be meaningful if we take into consideration the nature and complexity of the material, the needs and purposes of the reader and the adequacy of his understanding. We do not want to read rapidly simply for the sake of reading rapidly. We need to be able to read rapidly because in certain circumstances our needs and purposes are best met by rapid reading.

There is, unfortunately, no magic process by which huge blocks of words can be assimilated in visual gulps. The only claim made for this book is that it will show the advantages of efficient and rapid reading habits and how they may be established.

CHAPTER 1

How Well Do You Read?

IF you wish to improve your reading efficiency it is necessary to start by making some assessment of how accurately and how quickly you can understand printed pages. A complete reading course presents carefully graded reading exercises with comprehension tests, and the reader is required to time his reading, work out his score on the comprehension test and keep a record of his progress. In this book it is not possible to include sufficient exercises for the reader to chart his progress; but, nevertheless, it will be helpful if the exercises are timed, preferably with a stop watch, and a record made of the standard of comprehension.

The following reading passage attempts to answer the question "What is efficient reading?" Do not be put off by the fact that the reading is being timed. This is not the first heat in a reading race. Bear in mind only that you are reading this passage so that you can understand the information given in it.

Before you start reading make sure that you are sitting comfortably in a good light and that nothing is likely to distract your attention for a few minutes. Read the article as you would read a magazine or newspaper feature article whose title has interested you. At the end of the passage there is a comprehension test from which you will gain some idea of how accurately you have grasped the information set out in the passage.

Start Timing—What is Efficient Reading?

"Reading is a process in which our minds translate printed symbols into the ideas which the writer is trying to communicate to us. We do not really know what happens when we read a page of print, but in contrast with the extreme complexity of this visual and mental activity, the aim of reading is very simple. We read so that we may under-

I

stand. If we do not grasp the writer's meaning we cannot be said to have *read* the words at all. If we merely *look at* printed symbols and our minds do not register the amount of meaning we require, then we are wasting our time.

Reading efficiently means understanding pages of print accurately, rapidly and enjoyably. To do this the reader must acquire particular skills and techniques which he uses to suit his needs and purposes, and which he is able to adapt according to the nature and complexity of the material he is reading.

We do not just read. We read, or ought to read, always for a particular purpose, and, having decided on the purpose for which we are reading a particular piece of writing, we need to select the appropriate reading methods which will best achieve that purpose. This is a fairly obvious point, but one of the main differences between an efficient reader and an inefficient one is that the inefficient reader all too frequently fails to define adequately his purpose in reading, and consequently tends to treat all his reading matter in the same way. This puts him in the same class as a carpenter with one tool or a golfer with only one club. The efficient reader, on the other hand, always makes an assessment of what he wishes to achieve and then uses the reading methods appropriate to his needs.

Just as the way in which we read any printed matter depends on our purpose in reading, so the amount of comprehension that we will have gained when we finish is also determined by our purpose in reading. Reading is basically a process of *discrimination*, and, as understanding in accordance with the reader's needs and purposes is the sole aim of reading, the efficient reader must be able to differentiate between what is important to him and what is less important.

These points are to some extent summed up by saying that the efficient reader is the one who concentrates always on reading for meaning—or reading for ideas. Because he realises that he *must* understand what he is reading his concentration is always fixed on the task of getting meaning from the printed symbols and then, or simultaneously, selecting what he needs from this information. This means that the efficient reader is always deliberately and determinedly searching for the kind of information he requires.

If someone tells us to go into the garden and see if we can find anything, he is setting us a task without an ending. But if he tells us to go into the garden and find some strawberries we can do the job quickly, efficiently and enjoyably. It is the same with reading. If we do not adequately define our purpose in reading any material we are unlikely to read it efficiently. Without a clearly defined purpose we tend to swoop like magpies on every glittering object that appeals to our passing fancies and finish up by resembling Pope's

'Bookful blockhead, ignorantly read
With loads of learned lumber in his head.'

One of the fundamental maxims of efficient reading must therefore be, 'Knowing what you are looking for will always increase the possibilities of finding it quickly and accurately.' In fact our ability to learn depends primarily on our ability to ask questions, understand the answers and relate the relevant new knowledge to our previous knowledge. In reading (on which, incidentally, most of our learning depends) the fundamentals of efficiency are, therefore, the ability to define correctly our purposes in reading, to learn how to ask relevant questions, to read for meaning, to think as we read, and to select and relate the information we gain.

These matters have been mentioned first because in the rush of modern life a great deal of emphasis is sometimes laid on speed in reading without connecting speed with the all-important matter of comprehension. Speed in reading can never be an end in itself and it is important *only* in so far as it can sometimes assist the reader in getting the information he requires as accurately as possible.

The efficient reader has no fixed reading speed. Sometimes, if the passage he is reading demands intensive and critical study, his average speed may be less than 100 words a minute. At other times, when he is reading familiar material and needs only to isolate the main ideas, he may be skimming the material at well over a thousand words a minute. In short, the efficient reader adapts his speeds and methods to suit his needs and purposes in reading the particular kind of material he has in front of him.

The main factors in speeding up reading have to do with the way our minds work rather than with the way our eyes move over the lines of print. We can, however, help ourselves to become more efficient readers by knowing something of what our eyes do when we read. A film of the eye movements of a poor reader will show that in order to read a line of print his eyes fixate momentarily and unrhythmically on each individual word in the line and sometimes even on the syllables. His eyes also occasionally regress, that is, dart backwards to look again at some word he thinks he has missed. The efficient reader, on the other hand, usually takes in an average line of print in three (or at most four) rhythmical eye movements and rarely regresses.

From a physical point of view it follows that by taking in more words at a glance (and consequently making fewer pauses in each line) we shall not only read faster but also expend less energy. How can we learn to do this? Some help can be gained from perception exercises designed to quicken up responses and by exercises in reading groups of words as quickly as possible in a single glance. But it is probably more true to say that a reader with good eye movements has them because he is an efficient reader, than to say he is an efficient reader because he has good eye movements.

One reason why this is so is that the efficient reader reads for meaning, and single words do not convey much meaning until they are linked with other words. When an efficient reader takes in a line of print in three fixations the important thing is that he is taking in at each glance a meaningful group of words. Because of this he is not particularly conscious of the individual words but concentrates instead on the meaning they convey when connected together in groups. Correct eye movements are, therefore, not only physically economical but also necessary to fulfil the aim of any reading which is to get the meaning. By learning to get meaning quickly and accurately we learn almost incidentally to make the correct eye movements.

The efficient reader reads word groups but his understanding depends basically on the fact that he has a very extensive knowledge and appreciation of individual words. Vocabulary work must always be the first essential for efficient reading, but much more is involved than a mere knowledge of a large number of words. In order to understand, the reader must think as he reads. Thinking is obviously an integral part of reading, but the point is emphasised here because it is not always realised that words are essential for accurate thought, and so the reader, particularly when he is reading any unfamiliar material, must have at his command an extremely wide variety of words. Knowledge of words is not enough. There must be a complete familiarity with individual words before the reader can hope to react readily to the whole meaning of word groups.

Familiarity with an extensive range of words makes a reader less conscious of individual words. It allows his mind not only to grasp more readily the ideas which the word groups convey, but also teaches him not to rely on the sound of words in order to understand their meanings. The poor reader is almost always dependent on sound for meaning. The more inefficient the reader the more likely he is either to be aware of the actual sound of the words or, worse, to move his lips while reading. Before anyone can learn to read efficiently this sound barrier must be broken, otherwise the speed of reading will be inflexibly tied to the rate of pronunciation which is usually less than 200 words a minute —a very slow reading speed for all but the most difficult material.

Slow reading of uncomplicated material is extremely inefficient partly because it is tiring and frustrating, partly because it does not fully occupy the mind, and consequently the reader's attention has the opportunity to wander. If daydreaming is to be avoided the reader must learn to read at the maximum speed at which he can adequately assimilate material. There is a time for reading and a time for daydreaming, but if they are going to be combined neither will be done efficiently.

It is useless to tell anyone to avoid 'vocalisation' and 'inner speech'. In fact a conscious effort to overcome these disabilities frequently results in making matters at least temporarily worse. Probably the most effective way of over-coming defects such as inner speech and poor eye move-ments is by concentrating on reading for meaning and the *progression* of the ideas contained in the reading.

Reading is one aspect of communication. The reader who wishes to improve his efficiency will find it of value to con-sider the *two-way* process of communication from the writer's point of view. The reason for this is that reading is, in a sense, the reverse of writing, and every writer who is doing his job properly takes particular care to present his ideas in such a way that they become as easy to assimilate as the theme and subject matter permit. The writer attempts to make his material readable and it follows that the reading of it must become more efficient as the reader becomes more familiar with the various ways in which writers attempt to increase their 'readability'.

Most of these ways are familiar. The correct organisation of thought units such as paragraphs and sentences, the de-liberate placing of important words, effective connections, grammar and punctuation, are just as important to the reader as to the writer, although when we are at school such matters are more frequently mentioned in the context of writing than in the context of reading.

A complete familiarity with these various techniques en-ables the reader to sense rapidly the structure of any written material. This helps him to think about the subject matter in the same way as the writer did. The reader may not agree with the ideas put forward but he will know the writer's meaning, and his knowledge of the way in which the material has been presented will help the progression of the reading and also help him to differentiate between prin-cipal and subsidiary ideas.

Sensational claims of reading speeds of thousands of words a minute refer to the reading techniques generally known as skimming and scanning. Skimming is the tech-nique of picking out *only* the main ideas and ignoring *all* the subsidiary elements. Scanning is the technique of finding rapidly the answer to a particular question. Both are ex-tremely rapid methods of reading but obviously they have limited uses. We would skim, for instance, when we look rapidly through a book before reading it in detail. At other times we would skim when our purpose in reading is limited to getting only the main ideas, or when we are up against time and decide that a very general idea of the subject matter is preferable to complete ignorance. In circumstances such as these we do not need the details and can justifiably ignore them. The particular abilities needed for skimming have already been mentioned: the ability to distinguish accurately and rapidly between what is important and what is less important; and the ability to become involved in the author's thought and presentation by being aware of the way his ideas have been organised.

Scanning is the technique we all use, either efficiently or inefficiently, when we look up a word in a dictionary or a number or address in a directory. It can also be used to find any isolated fact in any kind of written material. The technique is largely a matter of sweeping one's eyes rapidly over the lines with the mind alert for the kinds of words that are likely to be used to express the information required.

These techniques are of immense value if they are used for particular purposes and according to particular needs. But when any kind of rapid reading technique is used it must be remembered that there is no point at all in reading rapidly simply for the sake of reading rapidly. Very rapid reading should only take place in particular circumstances where one's needs and purposes are best met by rapid reading.

We read to understand. If we bear this in mind every time we read we shall not only improve our reading efficiency but we shall also improve our ability to remember. Reading, as we have seen, is a process of discriminating between what we need and what we do not need, and between what is important and what is less important for any particular purposes. Memory, too, is selective, and consequently it is safe to say that the person who reads efficiently is the person who remembers efficiently, because both reading and remembering are concerned with selection and discrimination.

Efficient reading is above all the ability to read for meaning. It is important to bear this in mind when considering the problems of memory, because the most difficult facts to remember are isolated facts and the easiest facts to remember are those which are meaningful. It may not be possible to improve the *quality* of one's memory, but it is certainly possible to learn how to organise our powers of remembering in an efficient way. This we can do by learning and practising the skills and techniques of efficient reading because many of the problems and difficulties (such as those involving selection and making information meaningful) are of the same kind.

The two most difficult kinds of reading are, firstly, intensive reading which any studying involves; and secondly, critical reading in which we have to evaluate information as well as assimilate it. In these kinds of reading all the various skills and techniques may have to be used to give an amount of comprehension appropriate to the purposes, needs and methods of the reader. But, in addition, the reader's critical faculties must, whenever necessary, be brought into play to provide an accurate assessment of the information.

Study reading involves the use of a systematic though flexible approach which requires considerable ability in many different reading skills ranging from the ability to define one's purpose accurately to the techniques needed for the accurate reduction, rephrasing, reorganising and remembering of the information gained. In addition to this, good critical reading also requires the ability to think logically, to ask the right questions and to separate fact from feeling. The more varied the subject-matter the more the critical reader needs a wide general knowledge. It goes without saying that he should also be aware of the various techniques of persuasion and propaganda which are commonly used.

Much of what has been written in this article might seem too serious for the many people who read 'only for pleasure'. But why should not efficiency increase pleasure? Whether we read for pleasure or for necessity we still read in order to understand. And as learning to read efficiently means learning to understand efficiently it is reasonable to say that our pleasure in reading will be increased as our efficiency increases. The reader who reads for relaxation might say that the speed at which he reads is irrelevant, and that so long as he derives pleasure from his reading he is quite happy to continue at his own pace. But if such a person could be convinced that efficient reading techniques would enable him to read more quickly and accurately by expending *less* energy, surely he would agree that his pleasure must also increase.

There is in fact no reason for thinking that the use of efficient reading techniques takes the pleasure out of reading. On the contrary, evidence in a great variety of different spheres shows that pleasure usually increases as efficiency increases." Stop timing.

That passage contained about 2,800 words. Divide the number of words by the number of seconds it took you to read the passage, multiply by 60 and the result will give you your reading speed in words per minute: e.g. if the passage took 8 minutes 20 seconds, you have $\frac{2,800}{500} \times 60 = 336$ words a minute. Knowing your reading speed is no use at all unless the passage has been accurately understood. Reading, no matter how rapid, is a waste of time without adequate understanding. The title of the passage is "What is efficient reading?" and you were asked to read the passage in the same way as you would read a magazine or newspaper feature article whose title has interested you. If you have read the article efficiently you ought now to be able, without referring to the article, to answer the question "What is efficient reading?" or, to be more exact, "What does the writer of the article say the essential ingredients of efficient reading are?" For instance, he states early on that every reader ought to define his purpose in reading. Can you continue? This is the comprehension test: Write out in note form without referring to the article the distinguishing marks of an efficient reader.

When you have finished check the accuracy and completeness of your statement by referring to the article and then assess your comprehension in this way:

Very Good...No inaccuracies or omissions.

Good ....No inaccuracies but a few *minor* omissions.

Adequate ...Some *minor* omissions and/or inaccuracies.

Fair............Some *important* omissions and/or inaccuracies.

Poor ....A significant number of important omissions and/or inaccuracies.

An efficient reader would be able to read the article at about 400 words a minute with a comprehension grading of either good or adequate. If your own reading did not come up to this standard it is important to find out why not, because one of the necessities of self-instruction is self-criticism. As you assess the standard of your comprehension try to find where your reading weaknesses lie. Wherever there are important points in the text which you either omitted or misrepresented in your summary, try to say why you failed to remember them or to understand them correctly.

Here are a few questions which will help to make you aware of your reading weaknesses. Think carefully about each question in relation to your general reading as well as to the article you have just read, and try to discover your weaknesses. Answer each question Yes/No/Sometimes.

1. Do you read for a definite purpose?
2. When you have a definite purpose do you keep it clearly in mind as you read?
3. Are you particularly aware of paragraphs as you read?
4. In any given paragraph on a familiar subject can you distinguish rapidly and accurately between the main ideas and the supporting details?
5. After reading a chapter of a book or a complete article can you summarise in a connected and meaningful way the main ideas which have been presented?
6. After reading a book of general interest can you explain the gist of it to someone else?
7. Do you vary your speed of reading according to your purposes and the nature of the material?

8. Do you try to find the general theme and method of treatment of all your non-fiction reading so that you will be helped in reading the material more efficiently?

9. Are you always aware of the different styles of the writers you read?

10. While reading are you aware of questions arising in your mind?

11. Do you find that a knowledge of punctuation helps you to get the meaning accurately?

12. Do you find that a knowledge of grammar helps you to get the meaning accurately?

13. Can you understand the meanings of words without being conscious of their sound?

14. Can you read a fairly lengthy passage without regressing?

15. Are you able to concentrate on your reading without day-dreaming?

16. Can you read for long periods without your eyes feeling tired?

17. Are you interested in words, their meanings, etymology, etc.?

18. Are you less aware of individual words than the ideas they convey?

19. Do you think of yourself as a person with a very good vocabulary?

20. Do you read groups of words at one glance?

21. Do you think you have a good memory for what you read?

22. Do you feel confident when you tackle a difficult book dealing with an unfamiliar subject?

23. Do you regard reading as a necessary part of your life?

24. Do you regard yourself as a well-read person?

25. Do you enjoy reading?

Your answers to these questions will give you some idea of why your reading is not as good as it might be. An efficient reader would confidently answer "*yes*" to all the questions. What is important at the moment is to realise that if you are not satisfied with your ability to read quickly, accurately and with enjoyment, there are definite ways in which you can learn to improve. You will need determination and you will have to practise, but if you want to improve there is no doubt that you will improve.

The article you have just read should have given you a very general picture of what is meant by efficient reading. During the course of this book all the points mentioned in the article will be amplified and the various techniques discussed in greater detail.

CHAPTER 2

How To Improve Your Reading

PEOPLE who want to improve their reading fall into several different categories. There are professional and business people overburdened with reports and memoranda, needing to improve their reading efficiency to do their work more effectively, to keep up with current developments in their specialities and to give themselves more leisure time. There are frustrated readers who would like to be better informed, but for a variety of reasons find difficulty in realising their objectives. Then there are increasing numbers of students with heavy reading schedules to cope with; and leisure time readers who enjoy reading, and who believe, quite correctly, that if they could read and assimilate twice as many books with the same or even less effort they would derive twice as much enjoyment and benefit from their reading.

To which category do you belong? Perhaps you belong to more than one, or perhaps you have another reason for wishing to improve your reading. The motive itself does not matter. What does matter is that you should have a motive and should assess what it is worth to you in terms of time to improve your reading.

The way to efficient reading lies in acquiring a set of skills and habits. Some efficient readers acquire these by trial and error over the years and if asked how they read would probably be hard put to it to explain exactly what techniques they use. But trial and error is not a very sound basis for perfecting vital skills. We need to start out on a well-defined programme of work which is designed to build up effective reading habits.

How can we do this? The most important factor is motivation and the stronger the motivation the more quickly the skills are learned. The second most important factor is knowledge, because motivation without knowledge of what to do must inevitably lead to frustration. Because you are reading this book you must have a certain amount of motivation, and after reading the first chapter you should have a little general knowledge of the skills that are necessary for efficient reading. But this knowledge will not help very much unless you learn to acquire and then apply the necessary skills. Practice is the third important factor.

Efficient reading then is a combination of skills which must function together to produce the amount of comprehension which the reader needs for a particular purpose. Even though it is a *combination* it is possible to treat separately some of the most important skills, habits and abilities that make up the process of efficient reading. Here some of them are presented in the form of a list so that you may become familiar with them and have a preview of the topics that are dealt with in the remainder of the book. Some of them will already be familiar as they were mentioned in the self analysis at the end of the last chapter.

1. Establishing clearly the purpose of your reading.

2. Picking out the main thoughts and ideas of a passage and refusing to be side-tracked by less important or unimportant details.

3. Formulating questions as you read and looking in a determined way for the answers.

4. Relating new material to what is already known.

5. Flexibility in adapting speeds and techniques to your needs and purposes and to the difficulty of the material.

6. Being word conscious and developing a wide vocabulary.

7. Reading as far as possible in complete silence without even "saying the words aloud to yourself".

8. Reading with the minimum of eye movements for each line of print and reading word groups rather than individual words.

9. Locating and understanding key-words and key-phrases.

10. Finding the structure in any piece of writing.

11. Concentrating.

12. Remembering.

There is a great deal of difference between knowing what one ought to do and being able to do it. At the outset it is worth stressing the point about practice. Without practice theoretical knowledge is inadequate. A non-swimmer can read a hundred books about swimming, but unless he practices he is unlikely to survive for long when dropped into deep water. In the same way a poor reader will not be able to deal adequately with a difficult reading schedule merely by knowing how, in theory, he ought to set about it. Practice is of the utmost importance but it need not be a wearisome chore. Long, tedious sessions are unnecessary and unproductive. Permanent and effective improvement can be made by short, sure but regular steps. A little and often is the best guiding rule.

The goal you set yourself should be easily attainable. It is better to be able to increase the schedule than to be forced by pressure of work or other interests to decrease it. But whatever the schedule you set yourself, make a particular effort to keep to it.

Before going on to the other chapters in this book select a book on which you can practise the various skills that we shall discuss. The book should be non-fiction with a familiar vocabulary and on a subject which you find absorbing. Probably you have in mind a book which you have long been wanting to read. Now is the time to start it. Buy the book if possible—the fact that you have spent fifteen shillings on it will increase your motivation. If you do not want to buy the book get it from the local library. If it is not on the shelves, order it. But get it from somewhere.

If you have no particular book in mind browse around bookshops and libraries and consult periodicals such as *The Times Literary Supplement* or the book review pages of your newspaper or weekly magazine. Have a look at the Reader's Guide published by Penguin Books. This book contains over 1,800 descriptive recommendations of books in 18 different fields of knowledge. However you make your choice remember that it should be a book that you *want* to read and it should be written in a vocabulary with which you are familiar.

Set aside a particular period each day for reading this

book. It may only be half an hour. The exact length of time does not matter very much as long as you stick to it. Start reading the book as soon as you like, but before you begin bear in mind what you are doing. You are reading the book so that you may understand and remember the information which is contained in the pages. That is all. No one derives any pleasure from moving his eyes uncomprehendingly over lines of print. And if you are in the habit of reading only to avoid domestic duties ("No, dear, you can't play with Daddy now, he's reading") then this is not the book for you. There are several useful works on how to lead a peaceful life, but this is not one of them.

If the reading test in the previous chapter has made you worry about your reading speed, stop worrying. An efficient reader has different speeds for different purposes. Slow down or speed up as you consider necessary for the particular passage you are reading. Forget about eye movements. If your eye movements are poor, then it is because you are an inefficient reader; they will improve as your efficiency improves. If you are worried by your inability to understand or to recall what you have read, get into the habit of stopping after you have read a few pages or a chapter and practise summarising the main points you have read. If you cannot summarise them adequately it is important that you should ask yourself why this is so. Perhaps you have chosen a book that is too difficult or has too many unfamiliar words. Perhaps you are reading too slowly and giving your mind too much opportunity to digress. Or perhaps something distracted you and you lapsed into a day-dream. Whatever the reason for your failure in understanding, try to isolate it. Knowing why you have failed is the best starting-point for success.

The remedy for many failings in comprehension will be found in learning to concentrate on what you are doing. The book is open in front of you so that you can get information from the print. If you are not getting the information you are wasting your time. Adopt a more determined attitude to your reading. It may help you to imagine that someone is going to ask you some questions or discuss the chapter with you when you have finished.

Are you one of those readers who say the words "silently aloud" as you read? For the moment the best remedy for this fault is to concentrate on reading for the meaning. Try to discover the pattern of the author's presentation.

Here is a short reading exercise designed to help you to put into practice the main points about reading which we have mentioned so far. The passage is about weather forecasting, and was first published on World Meteorology Day in March 1961. These are the points about reading which you should bear in mind before starting to read the passage.

1. Be determined to get information from the passage. It is about weather forecasting and how the nations of the world co-operate in accurately forecasting the weather.

2. Concentrate on the main ideas. Try to get the information in proportion. Details tend to look after themselves provided that you fully understand the main points.

3. Do not regress, i.e. look back at what you have already read. Concentrate on progression.

4. Forget about speed, eye movements and vocalisation.

5. Make sure you are comfortably seated with a good light falling on the page and that you are free from distractions for a few minutes.

Time the reading of the passage, and when you have finished answer the questions that follow without looking back at the passage.

WEATHER FORECASTING

"Reasonably accurate weather forecasts are something taken for granted nowadays, at least wherever there are regular newspaper or radio services. Yet, not much more than fifty years ago, foretelling what the weather would do next was still for most people a matter of personal lore, superstition, tradition, or sheer guesswork. The complicated system on which we now rely had scarcely begun to be built up, although many countries had had good meteorological services for half a century or so. Now, we are so accustomed to the weather forecast as one of the conveniences of our daily life that very few people think twice about it, and even fewer have any idea of what goes into the making of the forecasts on which they rely, for business or pleasure, every day.

The basis of weather forecasting is the weather map and most people will, at some time or other, have seen such maps in newspapers or in television broadcasts or in other ways. These maps are of course simplified versions of the weather maps drawn at one of the forecasting offices of the country concerned.

The first thing one notices about a full weather map is that the geographical area covered by the map is much greater than the area for which forecasts have to be issued. This is of course because the weather travels with the wind and the forecaster therefore needs information from a very large area surrounding the place for which he is expected to forecast. It follows at once that an effective forecast service can only be maintained if there is international collaboration between the countries of the world in the exchange of weather information. The next point to notice is that if weather information is to be of maximum value for forecasting purposes it must be received promptly. Thus, for many years, the countries of the world have collaborated and have developed telecommunication systems by which weather reports are exchanged between countries, between regions, and even between continents. It is also, of course, necessary to have an efficient internal telecommunication system within each country for the rapid exchange of weather information.

All the modern telecommunication methods are used for meteorological purposes including, for example, radio-teletype and facsimile transmissions. The former is a system whereby the weather reports are transmitted by radio and are automatically typed out at the receiving station. The latter is a system whereby weather maps themselves are transmitted by radio or by landline and are automatically reproduced at the receiving station.

But, let us return again to the weather map. A close examination will show that over the region covered by the map, information is plotted in the form of figures and symbols, for each of a number of meteorological stations covering the whole region. Of course, where there is a sea area there are no stations, but arrangements have been made for merchant ships to send in reports and, in some cases, for special ocean weather ships to supply weather information from these areas.

The figures and symbols are the meteorologist's way of indicating measurements of such things as air temperature and humidity, atmospheric pressure, surface wind speed and direction, visibility, cloud types and amounts and heights, and so on. For some stations special observations of the upper atmosphere are made by small radio-transmitters attached to large hydrogen-filled balloons.

The reports from this network of surface and upper-air stations are the basis of the weather map and hence of weather forecasting; thus the question of the establishment and maintenance of an adequate national network of meteorological stations is of great importance in all countries.

On the basis of the information normally plotted on his map the forecaster, who is generally a highly skilled scientist, then draws series of lines which indicate various meteorological features. Surface isobars will show areas of high and low pressure, and hence, cyclones and anticyclones. Other lines will show areas of cold and warm air at various heights in the upper atmosphere, or will show the directions in which the upper winds are moving and their speed.

In most cases, the forecaster will then draw another set of charts showing the situation as he considers it will appear at some future time, for example, 12 or 24 hours ahead. These are usually called 'prognostic charts'.

Finally, on the basis of these charts, he will make his deductions as to what the forecast should be. For the general public, this may be forecasts of rain or sunshine; for the aviator, it may be a very detailed forecast of conditions for a particular flight; for the farmer, it will be a forecast of conditions for sowing or reaping of wheat or some other crop; for the sailor, it may be a gale warning or a fog warning.

While forecasting is still to a large extent a subjective process in which the maps and charts are aids to a mental process which results in the forecasters' predictions, modern technological advances have been applied successfully to the improvements of forecasts. The telecommunication systems just described are examples of this. The use of radio and radar techniques for detecting and watching the movement of rain areas and for measuring upper winds is another example. A more recent development has been the use of high-speed electronic computers to assist in weather prediction. Already in some countries these computers are being used to produce the prognostic charts referred to above, thus saving much of the time of the forecaster who previously prepared these charts by hand. What is more important, these prognostic charts are likely to become more accurate than those produced by subjective methods—indeed, in some countries this stage has already been reached for certain types of prognostic charts. There still remains of course the vital task of interpreting these prognostic charts in terms of rainfall at a particular time or place, or the wind at a height of 10 kilometres for a jet-aircraft, or a frost warning for a farmer, or a gale for a sailor. Thus, skilled forecasters will be a necessity for many years to come, if not for ever, and the use of modern technological advances does not in any way diminish the skill and training required for this work.

For the other types of meteorological work—for example, the persons who plot the weather maps, those who operate the radar and other equipment, those who take the meteorological observations at the many stations included in the network described above—special technical training is also required, but the nature and standard of training naturally depend upon the duties to be performed.

Recent developments in artificial satellites have an important bearing on weather forecasting. The possibility of taking photographs of cloud systems over large areas of the world's surface by means of satellites, and of taking other scientific measurements, suggests that, in the near future, a new and valuable technique will be available on a routine basis to assist the weather forecaster in his important work."

Published for Public Information purposes on the occasion of the First Annual World Meteorological Day, 23 March 1961 by the Secretariat of the W.M.O., Geneva, Switzerland.

The following questions on "Weather Forecasting" should be answered briefly in writing :

1. What do you know about weather forecasting fifty years ago?
2. Why is the geographical area covered by a full weather map much greater than the area for which the forecasts have to be issued?
3. Why are telecommunication systems between countries important in weather forecasting?
4. What are "facsimile transmissions"?
5. How are observations of the upper atmosphere made for weather forecasting purposes?
6. What are "surface isobars" and what do they show?
7. What is the technical term used for the charts which show the weather situation as it will appear at some future time, e.g. 12 or 24 hours ahead?
8. What three modern technological advances have been applied successfully to the improvement of weather forecasting?
9. Are modern technological advances likely to supersede skilled weather forecasters?
10. What effect are recent developments in artificial satellites likely to have on weather forecasting?

When you have jotted down brief answers to these questions look back at the passage and find out where, if at all, you have gone wrong. Nine or ten correct answers is good; eight, adequate; six or seven, fair; five or less, poor. The passage contains about 1,100 words. Work out your reading speed and make a note of it along with your comprehension grading.

If you were unsure of the answer to any question try to find out why you failed and then as you practise with the book you have selected try to remedy the faults. The main remedy for most reading weaknesses is in concentrating on reading for meaning. Read always in such a way that you can understand the information that the author is presenting. When you fail to understand try to pick out the fault. If you practise on these lines, poor reading habits such as undue regression, bad eye movements and vocalisation will tend to cure themselves though some specific practice and remedial work may be necessary.

A determination to get the information needed off the page and into your mind depends to a great extent on reading with a questioning mind, formulating questions as you read and looking deliberately for the answers. If you were reading "Weather Forecasting" in a determined manner you would automatically have formulated questions before and during the reading, and found the answers. Many of these questions would have been the ones set in the comprehension test. This is what is really meant by reading for meaning.

CHAPTER 3

Purpose in Reading

An inefficient reader usually fails to define properly his purposes in reading. Consequently, he tends to treat every piece of reading that he undertakes in more or less the same way. If the reader's purpose never varied he would, of course, have little reason to vary his techniques. But the needs and purposes for which we read vary with each different piece of reading and therefore our reading techniques should also be constantly changing so that we can always get the amount of understanding that we require.

Most people know this. For instance, let us imagine a football fan picking up an unfamiliar newspaper to find the result of a match. Does he start on page 1, column 1 and read methodically through the whole paper to find the report of the match? Never. Most football fans would find the report with almost magical speed whether it is on the back page or hidden away on page 4 or page 18. They can do this because their particular purpose in reading is absolutely clear to them. They may be fascinated by the Common Market or Bolivian politics, but if their purpose in reading the newspaper is to find the result of a football match, then they are not going to be side-tracked by any other issues whatsoever.

When the report has been located the way in which it is read will vary according to the purposes of the reader. The man who is not really interested in football but has laid a substantial bet on the result will get the information he wants in a second or two. All other information about the match will be irrelevant to his purpose. On the other hand, the football addict who was unable to attend the match will probably read and re-read the whole account from start to finish. He will almost certainly want to discuss the match later with his friends and will need to remember in considerable detail what he reads.

A man who actually played in the game reads the account

in a different manner. First he probably scans the report to see if he has been mentioned personally. He does this with great speed and accuracy even if he is the sort of man who finds reading any sort of book a form of hard labour. Then he probably reads the report through. If the article has poured scorn on his performance there is a strong likelihood that when he has finished reading he will have picked out quite rapidly every error the writer has made and every remark good or bad about the other players.

A different kind of reader might be the mother of the seventeen-year-old goalkeeper who was the hero of the match. Provided she does not handicap herself by over-anxiousness, her ability to pick out and remember the relevant information about her son could well be a model of rapid and efficient reading.

In all these instances efficient reading has taken place according to a variety of purposes. The instances are admittedly trivial and exaggerated, but nevertheless they do show the tremendous importance of motivation or purpose in reading. Provided that we have the necessary background to understand the information in the first place, reading efficiency depends largely on this vital factor. The whole thing is explained psychologically by saying that reading is basically a complicated stimulus-response process. The most important psychological factor is that understanding is the main response, and understanding depends largely on the correct preparation for the mental task we have to perform. This is sometimes referred to as getting the right mental set.

It is easy to define the differing mental sets of the readers of the football article. In each case the purpose of the reading was firmly defined and speed and accuracy resulted because other responses not relevant to the task were almost entirely eliminated. In all cases the main motivation was interest in the subject matter or some particular part of the subject matter of the article. And interest affects a person's reading performance more than any other single factor.

Before drawing any conclusions from this let us briefly study an everyday occurrence—the reading of a newspaper. Few people have either the time or the desire to read an entire newspaper every day. But people do not take a newspaper merely in order to pass the time, they take it so that they can be informed about what is happening in the world, and to add to their store of information about certain particular interests. The first job on picking up the newspaper is to select what is to be read and what can be left out. The newspaper is so arranged that the selection can be done by glancing at the headlines, which also to some extent reveal what reading methods will be necessary.

In front of me is a leader page from *The Guardian*. In the two left-hand columns are the leading articles and "A Country Diary". In the centre columns at the top is a feature article "Who Pays When the Police are Sued?" In the centre columns at the bottom are the letters to the editor. The right-hand column is taken up by the London Letter.

From previous experience of newspapers the kind of reading which each separate type of writing requires is obvious. The leading articles are mostly opinions and consequently they need to be read critically. This means that not only do we need to pick out the information presented but we also have to assess that information and form our own opinions about it. On this particular page the only leading article which interests me is one concerned with the ownership of newspapers. It is about 600 words long. Here is the actual article. Read it as you usually read a leading article whose subject interests you. Do not time the reading.

Owners of Newspapers

A congressional study of the "dwindling variety of news and comment" available in many parts of the United States is to be undertaken. This looks like being an inquiry parallel with that of the Royal Commission on the Press, which has been at work in Britain for some months. The British inquiry covers only the newspaper industry, while the American one is to deal also with radio and television. Both, however, are concerned with anti-trust laws. The congressional investigation is being undertaken by the anti-trust subcommittee of the Judiciary Committee of the House of Representatives. In Britain it is known that the Royal Commis-

sion has been considering anti-trust legislation as one possible means of maintaining
diversity of ownership and control among
newspapers.

In Britain, as in the United States, there
has been a marked trend towards concentration of ownership in the newspaper industry.
The Royal Commission was, indeed, ap-
pointed immediately after the struggle a year
ago for control of Odhams Press—a struggle
won by Mr. Cecil King's *Daily Mirror*
group against the opposition of Mr. Roy
Thomson.

American experience is of only limited
relevance here, both because American
newspapers are predominantly local in character and because the whole American
economy is already affected by anti-trust
laws. The provisions of the Sherman and
Clayton Acts apply to newspapers no less
than to other activities, and the Supreme
Court has dealt with a number of cases con-
concerning the press. How it would have dealt
with the acquisition of Odhams Press by
either the *Mirror* group or by Thomson
Newspapers is an exercise in imaginative
speculation. Conceivably it would have held
an acquisition by either party to be contrary
to the Clayton Act, and in that event presumably a "cease and desist" order would
have followed, leading to the separation of
Odhams from its new partner. Would this
have increased or decreased the *Daily
Herald's* chances of survival? Nobody can
tell. Such provisions have not prevented the
death of newspapers in the United States.
Indeed, the new congressional inquiry has
been spurred on by the recent reduction of
Los Angeles's daily newspapers from four
to two.

General anti-trust action in Britain does
not seem likely to come, but what of particular action in relation to newspapers?
The Royal Commission might recommend
this. If it were to do so, there seem to be
three possible approaches. One is legislation
setting precise limits to the size of newspaper groups. Parliament might, for example, be advised to lay down that no
individual or corporate body shall own or

control more than one national morning
newspaper and more than five (or ten or
fifteen) other daily newspapers. An excep-
tion might be made for existing holdings. A
second approach would be to amend the
Monopolies Act, 1948, so that morning and
evening newspapers can be considered separately under it. Then, if any group were to
exceed more than one-third of morning or
evening newspaper sales throughout the
United Kingdom, the Monopolies Commission could recommend remedial action. A
third way would be to amend the Act so
that one-fifth or one-sixth of the supply
from a single source became the test, instead of one-third. Morning and evening
papers could then be treated together and
ownership restricted if necessary.

Any of these steps would be open discrimination against the owners of large
newspaper groups, and as such perhaps ob-
jectionable. But by one of these methods
some social and political advantages might
be gained. Individuals could be prevented
from acquiring excessive political influence
through the purchase of newspapers; and
some companies would become immune to
"takeover" by stronger groups. Thus diversity of ownership might be preserved. None
of these steps, however, could save a newspaper under severe economic pressure
through lack of advertisements and insufficient sales. That is how death has come to
many, the *News Chronicle* among them.

How did you read the article? Did you start at the beginning and read through to the end? That would seem to be
the obvious approach, but is it the most effective and the
most economical in terms of time and effort? In order to
decide how best to approach the reading we need first of all
to define our purpose in reading. An efficient reader might
set about it this way. First, he knows that the article will
express an opinion about the subject, and it follows that if
he can find out what the main opinion is quickly and accurately he will be in a position to read the complete article
with a clearly defined mental set. Second, a main opinion is
frequently found as a conclusion, so it would seem more

realistic to read the end of the article first. The word "realistic" is used here because the efficient reader is not concerned with any conventional approach to reading, but only with getting the information off the page rapidly and accurately in such a way that he can understand that information and assess the opinions that are presented. He is concerned with efficiency and with economy and not with whether anyone thinks it peculiar that he should begin at the end or somewhere in the middle. The *result* of reading is what is important and if the reading is effective then the result will be adequate understanding.

The conclusion states: "Thus diversity of ownership might be preserved. None of these steps however, could save a newspaper under severe economic pressure through lack of advertisements and insufficient sales. That is how death has come to many, the *News Chronicle* among them."

In five seconds the efficient reader would learn that the writer believes that diversity of ownership can be preserved but that none of the possible steps are likely to be of much use if the paper is economically in the doldrums. He can now define his purpose in reading the article. He wants to know how the diversity of ownership might be preserved and so will read the article from the beginning in order to answer that particular question. As he reads the article other information might be of interest, and if it is he will formulate other questions and look for the answers. Finally, after considering the evidence given in the article and any other evidence he might have, he will be able to make some sort of assessment of the leader writer's opinion. How this can be done effectively is discussed in more detail in the chapter on Critical Reading.

The same principles can be applied to the feature article "Who Pays When the Police are Sued?" Before reading the article the purpose in reading it should be defined. This purpose must be to extract particular information and the more exact the reader can be about this required information the more efficient will his reading be. The article has a sub-heading which says "The second of three articles on the evidence presented to the Royal Commission on the Police." From these two headings the efficient reader can immediately formulate at least three separate but related questions. First, who *does* pay when the police are sued? Second, is this regarded as a satisfactory state of affairs? Third, what suggestions, if any, have been made for altering the situation? Other questions may arise during the reading of the article, but for the moment these questions are sufficient to ensure that the reader will extract the important information that he requires.

In the same way he would skim the other sections of the page—the Letters to the Editor and the London Letter— define his purpose in reading those parts that he decides to read, formulate questions wherever possible and then read the articles, deliberately looking for the answers to the questions. By tackling the reading in this way he will be unlikely to miss much that is important. When he has finished reading the page he will have extracted some particular information and because he found it by looking for it deliberately, he will stand a good chance of remembering it.

Much of what has been said so far in this chapter must be fairly obvious to anyone who does even a little regular reading. No apologies are made for stating the obvious, because it is a necessary preliminary to pointing out that the main difficulty in teaching people to read efficiently is to persuade them to put into practice what, if they think about it in a rational way, they know they ought to do. We come back then to the point about motivation. If you really want to read more efficiently the basis of the whole thing can be expressed in the phrase "Read for Meaning," and in order to get the meaning from the printed symbols it is necessary to make a preliminary survey of the material in order to define one's purpose, to formulate specific questions wherever possible and then to look deliberately for the answers. Other questions may form during the reading and additional answers may be looked for, but the reader should guard against "magpie reading", that is picking up every glittering piece of information that happens to catch his eye. Reading is a process of selection and discrimination, not of wholesale absorption.

Apart from the book suggested in the last chapter the best regular practice that you can do at the moment is with the daily newspaper. You do not, presumably, buy it to have a plentiful supply of waste paper about the house. You buy it because it contains information which is of value and interest to you, and as a reader it is your job to assimilate and remember a selection of that information. So each day practise reading in the way outlined above, adapting the method to suit your own particular needs and purposes.

Study the paper you read. Notice how news items are presented with the important information at the beginning and the details tailing off into insignificance at the end. Practise formulating questions from headlines, looking for the answers, summarising the information given and recalling at odd moments what you need to remember.

For a little more formal practice in this all-important matter of defining one's purpose and looking for specific information here is an extract from Professor H. J. Eysenck's *Sense and Nonsense in Psychology*. There are no headlines or sub-headings here to help us. But there is an introductory sentence which gives us a good idea of the subject matter.

"In recent years there has been a considerable degree of criticism of selection, particularly at the 11-plus level, and it is worth while to have a look at the most common of these objections."

With such an introduction we can safely assume that the passage is concerned with examining the most common objections to selection tests, in particular the 11-plus. We can therefore begin by asking the straightforward question: "What objections are there to selection tests and in particular the 11-plus?" We know that we shall find the answer to this question because the introductory sentence has told us so. But having found out what these objections are, we shall, if we are really interested in the subject, want to know whether these objections are valid or not. The introductory sentence does not tell us whether or not we shall find the answer to this second question in the passage, but we must bear it in mind.

Have these two questions in mind as you read the passage and then, when you have finished, see if you can answer them. Write down the answers as briefly as possible in your own words and then look again at the passage to see if you are correct. Time the passage but bear in mind that the important thing is to get the information you want from the passage. When you have checked your answers to the questions work out your reading speed and give yourself a comprehension grading in the same way as before.

From *Sense and Nonsense in Psychology*
by H. J. EYSENCK

"In recent years there has been a considerable degree of criticism of selection, particularly at the 11-plus level, and it is worth while to have a look at the most common of these objections. It is argued, for instance, that many children are so anxious on the occasion of the test that they do not do themselves justice. It is argued again that coaching produces a considerable effect on test scores, and that therefore the results are worthless. It is argued that the age at which selection takes place is too early in the life of a child, and that either no selection should take place at all, or that some form of 'streaming' should be introduced, with the constant possibility of changing the child from one stream to another. Whatever the objection, the argument usually ends by saying that intelligence tests are either useless or actively malfeasant in their influence.

Much of this argument arises from a very praiseworthy desire to give all children an equal chance, and to act on the principle that all men are created equal. Unfortunately, the facts make it quite certain that all men are not created equal, and that heredity clearly discriminates between the bright and the dull. In fact, the more we equalize the opportunities of education, the greater will be the influence of heredity in determining the final intellectual status of each child. This point is often argued by Communists, whose strange dogma seems to favour the conception of human beings as emerging with perfect uniformity from some conceptual conveyor belt, but no such view can be maintained for one moment in the face of the evidence.

Given innate differences in ability, we must next stress a fact which again has ample experimental foundation, namely that teaching is much more effective when the members of the class are of relatively uniform ability. It has often been shown that to teach the same material to a group containing bright, average, and dull members takes considerably longer and is considerably less effective than teaching the same material to a group consisting only of bright, or average, or dull members. It might, at first sight, seem surprising that it should be easier to teach a dull class than one of average ability, but the answer, of course, is that with a dull class the teacher can adapt himself and his methods to the level of his students, while with a class of average ability, containing both bright and dull students, the same methods of teaching simply will not be applicable to all members of the class, so that time-wasting duplication is necessary. Unless, therefore, we want to have highly inefficient teaching, we must segregate—quite apart from the fact that certain subjects at a reasonably advanced level are quite unsuitable for children with low I.Q.s.

Given that for those, as well as for many other reasons, some form of segregation is desirable, is eleven too early an age at which to estimate children's abilities? Follow-up studies have usually shown that there is very little overlap between the abilities of children in grammar and in modern schools, even when they reach the age of fifteen or sixteen, so that prediction in the vast majority of cases appears to have been remarkably accurate. What, then, about the criticisms of coaching and examination nerves? Both are justified, but they are criticisms, not of psychological tests and psychological theory, but of political and social pressures which prevent the best use being made of available knowledge. There is ample evidence that coaching produces a rise in I.Q. of about ten points or so, which is quite a considerable increase. It has also been shown, however, that simply giving children a few hours' practice in doing intelligence tests has much the same effect as coaching, and brings them to a point beyond which no coaching and no practice is found to increase their scores. The answer to the coaching problem, therefore, is quite a simple one. All children should be given five hours of practice on tests of intelligence before the crucial test is taken. This would counteract the effects of any coaching they would be given additionally, and give them all the same start. At the same time, this would reduce nervousness due to having to face an entirely new experience.

It would be preferable in many ways to have these five hours of testing spaced throughout the child's school period from six to eleven so that some knowledge could be gained at the same time of his intellectual growth pattern, because this might be of considerable value in making any predictions. Also it would reduce the importance of any particular single test, and would thus again have some effect in reducing examination nervousness. Children who did not come up to their expected level could be re-tested individually to determine whether this failure was due to nervousness or other extraneous causes. There are other ways in which the experienced psychologist could help education committees to overcome the difficulties involved in the administration of testing programmes and obviate the criticisms mentioned. Why, then, is nothing of this kind done?

The reason is a very simple one. If it costs 9d. per child to give one test of intelligence and score it, then it would cost almost 4s. to give five tests. The decision that a child's future happiness is worth only 9d. rather than 3s. 9d. is not made by the psychologist, but by the general public through their elected members of local government bodies. All one can say is that for 9d. the public is getting quite incredibly good value for its money. To have a fairly superficial examination of a car carried out costs several pounds. A reasonably complete health examination costs at least as much. To get a child's intelligence investigated for 9d. can hardly be considered an extravagant expenditure. The degree of accuracy of this measurement, of course, is directly dependent on the amount of money spent on it. The higher the degree of accuracy required, the more money will have to be spent on the examination. During my recent visit to California I was shown a large series of laboratories constructed at a cost of several million dollars for the sole purpose of getting a few thousandths of one degree nearer to absolute zero temperature! Our society is willing to pay large sums of money like this for a slight increase in the accuracy of physical measurement, but it is content with an expenditure of 9d. a child in the measurement of a psychological variable of great importance to both the child and society.

It is not my purpose in making this comparison to say whether this social decision is right or wrong. It is my purpose rather to point out some of the facts of the situation, and to show that if the accuracy of the measurement performed of a child's ability at the age of 11-plus is not all it might be, and is subject to various types of criticism, then it is not the psychologist who should be blamed, but society itself. By refusing to spend money on research, or refusing to implement the finds of private research because of a slight increase in cost, society has made a decision which may or may not be a correct one, yet discussion in the Press heaps all the resulting blame on the head of the psychologist for not performing miracles at the price of 9d., and fails to put before the public the facts of the situation so that it may have a chance to reconsider its verdict."

A Note on Physical Conditions

It was said earlier on in this chapter that purpose or motivation is of first importance in learning to read efficiently. But in these preliminary stages it must also be stressed that actual physical conditions greatly affect one's reading efficiency and that these physical conditions vary from person to person and even from purpose to purpose. It is therefore essential that anyone who wishes to read efficiently should experiment to find what physical conditions suit him best for the various kinds of material he has to read.

It is surprising how many people think that they can read with maximum efficiency ten feet from a television screen or fail to realise that constant telephone calls are unlikely to assist either concentration or comprehension. The more important points which affect everyone may be summarised as follows :

1. There should be sufficient intensity of light. Daylight is best for reading but as ideal conditions are not usually available it is generally accepted that the best illumination is a fairly powerful frosted bulb in a shaded lamp throwing the light over the left shoulder in such a way that there are no shadows.

2. There should be no distractions. There are as many different kinds of distractions as there are different kinds of reading material, but usually they can be got rid of by temporary exclusion, immobilisation or removal (either of the distraction or the reader). A distracted reader cannot be an efficient reader.

3. The seating conditions should be such that distractions do not arise either through discomfort or through too much comfort. They should also give the maximum ease in handling the material to be read. These conditions vary enormously from person to person. For instance, when doing intensive study reading in the evenings many people find that sitting at a table on a straight-backed chair provides the conditions for maximum efficiency. Others favour lying down on a bed. The only way to find out what suits oneself best is to experiment and to use one's common sense, always bearing in mind that the object of the exercise is to extract information from print with the maximum accuracy, speed and enjoyment.

CHAPTER 4

Comprehension: Reading for Meaning

"The people I want to send on this course are extremely busy men. They aren't interested in any of the frills of reading, they're just interested in speed. If my managers could all learn to read at eight or nine hundred words a minute they would probably be at least three times as efficient in their work." This extraordinary statement was made by a successful business man and it illustrates quite a number of the mistaken ideas which some people have about the skills of efficient reading.

The first thing that needs emphasising is that speed is not a value in itself, it is a tool of comprehension. If we accept that the aim of all reading is understanding, then we cannot talk about "speed" and "comprehension" in any meaningful way as though they were separate factors. If the reader does not assimilate the amount of meaning that he requires for his purposes, then he cannot be said to have *read* the material.

All the different skills and techniques of reading which are contained in this book are there solely to assist the reader to understand what he is reading at a level which fits in with his purposes, needs and methods. The efficient reader is the person who understands accurately and rapidly what is printed on the page. To do this effectively, whatever the kind of reading material, all these various skills and techniques must be learned so that they function automatically and the speed of reading relates always to the amount of comprehension needed. Anyone therefore who is concerned about speeding up his reading—that is, getting the thought off the page faster than he is accustomed to—must realise that what he needs to increase is his *speed of comprehension*.

How can this be done? It is largely a matter of hard work which will result in the development of good habits, the elimination of bad ones and the removal of any psychological hindrances. There is no easy way, but the work can be made less arduous by knowing what sort of practice is needed and how it should be done. Merely *knowing* the technique is insufficient. Practice is also essential.

To tie the matter down to particular considerations we can say that the development of faster comprehension depends basically on learning to read so that the ideas become of more importance than the words, and then learning to separate the important ideas from the less important ones, thus getting the material in proper perspective.

Many people, when they finish reading a passage, are unable to summarise the main points mentioned. Their reading seems to be a process of dredging miscellaneous items of information from the paragraphs and then leaving the whole lot unsorted in their minds. Given time they can sometimes arrive at a reasonably accurate summary, but "efficiency" is not a word that can be used in connection with their actions.

One important reason for this kind of inefficiency lies in the person's attitude towards words. Words are not in *themselves* of much importance. They are symbols, and the important thing about them is the ideas which they convey when they are grouped together. To the skilful reader a word is a unit of an idea and this means that, as he reads, he is unconsciously selecting important words from the lines of print, rejecting those words which are unimportant for his purpose and then grouping the "idea words" together.

Here, to illustrate the point, is a paragraph taken from the *Times Educational Supplement* (4 May 1962).

Cheeseparing on Books

"Our spending on education is astronomical. Our spending on school books is minute. Every set of relevant figures proves the point. The charge nowadays on the public purse for a primary child will be about £60 a year. For a sixth former it will be £100 more. Yet books for the one will scarcely reach £1; for the other they will take but a few shillings more. In 1960-61 our total spending on primary and secondary schools ran to £473 M. At £7,400,000 school books accounted for 1·6 per cent of this."

The paragraph contains 88 words. The slow, inefficient reader would probably read them all. In contrast, the efficient reader, although he will *see* all the words, will in fact *read* only about half of them. But, it may be said, if he reads only half the words he is likely to miss half the points, particularly in a newspaper or periodical where the whole thing is carefully edited so that no space is wasted. Is this really so? Let us look again at the paragraph and see if any vital information is lost when we cut out half the words. These are the words, arranged as groups of "idea words" which the efficient reader would actually *read* :

   spending on education astronomical   on school books minute   relevant figures proves point   charge nowadays on public   for primary child about £60 a year for sixth former £100 more   books for one scarcely reach £1   for other few shillings more   1960-61 spending on schools £473 M.   books accounted for 1·6 per cent.

The main idea stated in the paragraph is that we spend a lot on education but only a very small proportion of the money is spent on books. Reading the paragraph as a series of idea groups is in this case quite adequate.

It is not suggested that every kind of reading material can be treated in this way and reduced to half its word length without losing any of the meaning. The point is that in any sentence some words are of more importance than others because the meaning they convey is of more importance. Even a poor reader does not linger over articles or pronouns as much as he does over nouns and verbs. And any one who has attained any sort of proficiency in reading probably *sees* but does not *read* something between a quarter and one-third of the words on the pages.

This method of reading breaks up the word-by-word flow of the material and consequently its uses as a reading technique are limited to any uncomplicated kind of reading which can easily be absorbed. A lawyer reading a legal document would not, of course, use this method of reading. Nor would a student faced with any technical material designed for intensive study.

On the other hand everyone ought to be able to read in this way. It is for instance the most effective way of reading most of the articles or reports in a newspaper or in any kind of book where you are interested primarily in the writer's main ideas and not in the details. The sort of book which you were recommended to choose in the last chapter will probably be of this kind.

Mastery of the technique depends on practice. The technique might be described as the ability to select from the lines of print only those words which convey the thought clearly and economically. The secret of it is to learn to *think* while you read, that is to develop the ability to sense the structure of the passage and to involve yourself with the writer so that you can follow the way his thoughts progress. Your purpose in reading a book where the details are not of particular importance is to understand the writer's basic message as quickly and clearly as possible. This means that you have to understand and react to the relationship between the various parts of the material without losing yourself in a maze of detail. The details, which exist almost always to add various kinds of impact to the basic points that the writer seeks to put over, must be put into a proper perspective.

Reading for meaning, then, implies that the reader must search deliberately for the writer's main ideas. While practising this with the newspaper or the book you have selected you will find that habits of regression will generally cure themselves if you concentrate on progressing from main idea to main idea.

As you read for meaning, bearing in mind the distinct purpose you have, you will also find that after a short while you are no longer in the unfortunate position of being incapable of stating clearly what the book is about. When you reach that stage (which will be quite soon) you ought, if you wish to become an efficient reader, to make every effort to read more, to read widely and to read always with a definite purpose.

No matter why you want to be an efficient reader this practice on a wide variety of interesting books with a familiar vocabulary is an essential part of the necessary practice. As has been said before, this need not, and should not, be in any way a wearisome chore. A lot of reading can be accomplished in a regular hour a day divided up into two half-hour periods. But let it be reading, not just dozing over a book. If you wish to doze, then do so, but do not confuse the activity with reading. The efficient reader has time for day-dreaming as well as for reading, but he does not combine the two.

When you establish a routine for reading there are other points to practise in these preliminary stages at the same time as you learn to pick out the main ideas. First, practise reading under some pressure. When you have looked rapidly through a book and decided you would like to read it, make an assessment according to the level of difficulty involved of how many hours it ought to take you to read the book, plan your reading in relation to the time you wish to spend each day and then keep to the time set.

Second, practise concentrating. During the time set aside for reading—read. The more you can eliminate distractions during your reading session the sharper your understanding will become and this will result quite quickly in a definite increase in speed. But distractions must be eliminated. If you are at home choose a half-hour or an hour for reading when you are not required to pay the milkman, keep an ear open for the baby or turn the oven off. If you are at the office, get someone else to attend to the telephone; put a placard on the door; appeal to your secretary's protective instincts—but do something about distractions so that for a particular period each day you know that you can be alone with your reading.

Third, as you read, get into the habit of varying your reading speed as the kind of material changes. This might change from paragraph to paragraph or from chapter to chapter. Adapt your reading speed to the kind of material and to your purpose in reading. Speed up when you can and slow down if you have to. Flexibility is the mark of the efficient reader.

Fourth, practise summarising in your own words from time to time the main points which the writer has made. Bearing in mind that you are going to do this will help you to think as you read and to follow the writer's line of thought. If you summarise the main points well it will also help you to remember what you read. If you feel that your ability to summarise is inadequate, write down the summary and then check all the points looking for omissions and mis-representations and try to find out how the faults arose.

Here is an extract from Richard Hoggart's *The Uses of Literacy* in which he gives a thumbnail sketch of a working-class father. As you read it you will find that each paragraph provides one or more main facts about the working-class father. These main facts are reinforced by examples, subsidiary details and explanations. Your purpose in reading the passage is to pick out the main facts and to remember them. This does not mean that you are to ignore the examples and subsidiary details. It means that you must sort out the information so that it registers on the mind in a proper perspective, thus enabling you to pick out and retain the *main facts*. Having read the passage you ought then to be able to recall these main facts and at the same time to remember the examples and subsidiary facts which are there to reinforce the main facts and which have little value on their own. Your reading then should be concentrated first on the idea words and then on the main ideas that the words add up to when they are formed into meaningful groups.

The aim in reading this passage is *not* to get through it as quickly as possible but to ensure that when you have finished you will have assimilated accurately the main information given. Unless you can do this properly speed is of no use. But when you can do it properly you will find that your ability to do it rapidly has increased enormously.

As you read the passage concentrate on progressing from main fact to main fact. Look for idea words. Do not regress. You want to know what information Richard Hoggart has to give about working-class fathers. Look deliberately for this information and when you have found it get it in proportion. Do not waste time on inessentials. Time the passage in the same way as before.

From *The Uses of Literacy*

by RICHARD HOGGART

"Father.

Like his wife, a working-class man often seems to me almost physically recognisable. He tends to be small and dark, lined and sallow about the face by the time he has passed thirty. The bone-structure of the face and neck then shows clearly, with a suggestion of the whippet about it. In general, these physical marks are observable early, and remain throughout life. Thus—though this is lightly put—if I or some of my professional acquaintances who were born into the working-classes put on the sort of flat cap and neckerchief which go with looking "county", or if we leave our collars open, the sit of the cap and the neckerchief, or the structure of the bones round the neck, make us look, not like the sporting middle-class, but like working-men on a day off.

The point of departure for an understanding of the position of the working-class father in his home is that he is the boss there, the "master in his own house". This he is by tradition, and neither he nor his wife would want the tradition changed. She will often refer to him before others as "Mr. W." or "the mester". This does not mean that he is by any means an absolute ruler or that he gets or expects his own way in everything. It often accompanies a carefulness, a willingness to help and be "considerate", to be "a good husband". In the lazy or insensitive, it may support a considerable selfishness or near-brutality. In either case, there is likely to be a deference to him as the main breadwinner and heavy worker, even though these assumptions are not always correct today. He remains the chief contact with the outer world which puts the money into the house.

There is often a kind of roughness in his manner which a middle-class wife would find insupportable. A wife will say how worried she is because something is amiss, and "the mester will be mad" when he gets home; he may "tell yer off" harshly or in a few cases may even "bash" you, especially if he has had a couple of pints on the way from work. Or middle-aged wives will say to a younger one, "e's good to yer, i'n't 'e?", meaning that he is not likely to become violent in word or act, or that he does not leave his wife alone almost every night, or that he will "see 'er out" if she gets into difficulties with the housekeeping allowance. This is in part a heavy peasant crudeness in personal relations and expression, and clearly does not necessarily indicate a lack of affection, or a helplessness on the wife's part. The man who is able to growl is also able to defend; he has something of the cock about him. Hence, rough boys are often admired; the head-shaking over them is as proud as it is rueful—" 'e's a real lad", people say.

A husband is therefore not really expected to help about the house. If he does, his wife is pleased; but she is unlikely to harbour a grudge if he does not. "When all's said and done", most things about a house are woman's work: "Oh, that's not a man's job," a woman will say, and would not want him to do too much of that kind of thing for fear he is thought womanish. Or the highest praise will take the form, " 'E's ever so good about the 'ouse. Just like a woman": if he does help much he is doing it in place of the woman whose job it should be; the household chores are not joint responsibilities.

So it is a positive act of helpfulness if he decides to help with washing up or the baby. In many cases a wife would not only "never dream" of having his help with the washing, but does not feel that she can " 'ave the washing around" when he is at home. There are often difficulties of drying-space, especially on rainy days, that are aggravated by the need for a complicated system of putting the damp stuff round the fire on a clothes-horse and taking it off again into a basket or zinc bath at the times when the husband wants to "see t' fire".

There are many husbands who regard all the family's money affairs as a shared concern, who hand over their wage-packet on Friday night and leave its disposition to their wives. But an assumption just as characteristic, in my experience, is that the wage-packet is the husband's, and that he gives his wife a fixed amount for housekeeping each week. There are many households where the wife does not know how much her husband earns. This does not necessarily mean that she is poorly treated. "Oh, 'e sees me alright," or " 'e treats me alright," she will say, meaning that she is not left short but implying, in the phrasing itself, that the distribution of the wage lies with him. The wife is often responsible, out of this fixed amount, for any replacements—of crockery, furnishings, and so on; the more thoughtful of these husbands will be open to suggestion, will promise something out of the next payment of overtime. Quite often the wife's share of any overtime money only arrives quixotically. Sometimes she feels unable to discuss family financial problems with her husband, and this may extend even to such a question as whether it is possible to send a child to the grammar-school. There will be discussion of a kind, and particularly if it has to be decided whether a child can be kept at a grammar-school after sixteen, but it is not usually a precise discussion of financial ways and means, of how this can be cut here or that pleasure reduced there.

If he is on the dole, and the same assumptions naturally apply whether he is in that position through ill health or ill luck or shiftlessness, both husband and wife assume that he must still have his pocket-money. Self-respect is involved; "a man can't be without money in 'is pocket"; he would then fell less than a man, feel "tied to" his wife and inferior to her, and such a situation is against nature. He must have money for cigarettes and beer, perhaps even for an occasional bet, the amount regularly spent each week, even by men out of work, would seem in many cases excessive to, say, the professional middle-classes. Fifteen cheap cigarettes a day seems normal, and those cost about thirteen shillings a week; for a man out of work and drawing the dole, one pound a week for pocket-money is the figure I most commonly hear nowadays. Such things as cigarettes and beer, it is felt, are part of life; without them, life would not be life; there are rarely any other major interests to make these pleasures less relevant and worth forgoing. It is, I suppose, the sense that such things are part of the minimum staple of life which makes many families, even where the husband is working well and has plenty of money in his pocket, maintain the old arrangement whereby the wife buys "with the groceries"—that is, out of the housekeeping money—a proportion of the husband's weekly cigarettes.

I noted that girls are usually indulged by parents, but that, especially before they leave school, they are expected to do more about the house than their brothers. A boy soon acquires something of the feeling that "it's different for men" which he will have in greater strength when he is grown up. On leaving school the attitude quickly strengthens; he is, probably for the first time, close to his father and finds his father ready to be close to him; they now share the real world of work and men's pleasures.

All this is still largely true and must be put first, but has much too strongly implied that the husband is selfish and leaves all the troubles to his wife. The basic assumption is that the man is master of the house. Some of the expressions of this assumption, and these not the more unusual ones, might seem grossly unfair to the women. Yet there are a great many husbands who are thoughtful and helpful, who spend much of their free time at home, making and mending. Even so, there is the sense that the father occupies a special position. There are some things, difficult and men's things—such as chopping wood—which only he can do; there are others which he may do without undermining the order, such as getting himself off to work or bringing his wife a cup of tea in bed occasionally.

Among some younger husbands there are signs of a striking change in the basic attitude. Some wives press for it and find their husbands ready to modify the outlook they inherited from their fathers. Here as elsewhere, no doubt, educational improvements are quietly but pervasively promoting a different attitude among those who are ready to be affected. More particularly, a few husbands and wives may be influenced by the example of some young professional and lower-middle-class husbands who have learned, especially since the war, to help their wives as partial substitute for the daily help their class can no longer always afford. Some working-class husbands will share the washing up if their wives go out to work, or will take turns with the baby if their job releases them early and not too tired. But many wives come home from work just as tired as their husbands and "set to" to do all the housework without help from them. And not many working-class husbands will help their wives by pushing the baby round the streets in its pram. That is still thought "soft" and most wives would sympathise with the view.

If a wife has a conscious wish, it is probably not for a husband who does such things, but rather for one who remains a husband in much the old sense, yet "a good one" in the old sense, for one who is "steady" and "a good worker", one who is not likely to land her suddenly in poverty, who is likely to be kept on if sackings begin, who brings home his money regularly, who is generous with his bonuses.

Emotionally, his best contribution is to be, without being soft or "womanish", ready to agree, to live according to the idea that happy married life is "a matter of give and take". A great many, perhaps most, husbands do this: the working-class people have a host of jokes about marriage, but not against marriage. They are not harassed by the ambivalences of some more self-conscious people who are so shocked at the thought that they may end up in the bourgeois satisfaction of their parents that it takes them years to realise that they like being married, and even enjoy its ordinary duties and everyday necessities. Working-class men and women still accept marriage as normal and "right", and that in their early twenties. What a husband is earning at twenty-one, he is likely to be earning at fifty-one; he probably married a girl from exactly his own class, and they set about "getting a home of their own together" and living their lives inside it."

Can you now sum up the main information that Richard Hoggart has given us about the working-class father? The following questions are intended to be a guide to help you to do this.

1. What physical characteristics does Hoggart note in the working-class man?

2. What is the working-class father's position in the home?

3. What is said about his personal relationships with his wife in

(a) His general attitude towards his wife?
(b) His attitude towards household chores?
(c) His attitude towards money?

4. In what way does Hoggart think that a change in the basic attitude of the working-class father is taking place among many younger husbands?

5. How would you sum up the working-class attitude towards marriage?

Check the answers to the questions by referring back to the passage and then give yourself a comprehension grading of Good, Adequate, Fair, or Poor based on the omissions and misrepresentations, if any, that you made. Imagine that you are marking someone else's work as objectively as possible. If you are not completely satisfied with the comprehension then you cannot give a grading of Good or Adequate.

Whenever you find omissions or misrepresentations in your comprehension try to decide why you failed and resolve to concentrate on the particular faults that are holding you back. Always remember that if you have got one main fact correct there is nothing to stop you from getting all the main facts correct. Now that you know what you are doing and how to do it success is largely a matter of practice.

CHAPTER 5

What Happens When We Read

A LOT of the confusion about the skills of rapid reading arises out of the fact that many people when they think about reading tend to regard it as a purely visual process. "If only", they say, "I could read more words at a glance, whole sentences, whole paragraphs or even whole pages, I should be able to get through my reading in a fraction of the time." This sounds perfectly reasonable, but it must be remembered that we read with our minds as well as with our eyes and that even without any special training in perception we are already capable of *seeing* more in a glance than our minds can properly assimilate.

Our eyes merely transmit the visual impulses to the brain and then the whole complex process of interpretation and reaction begins. To become efficient readers we have to be more concerned with the interpretation and the response than with the transmission. Faulty transmission is a job for an eye specialist. From the point of view of reading it has to be stressed that there is no point at all in being able to see a great expanse of print in a single glance unless we are capable of interpreting it accurately and quickly. To repeat what has been said before and what is going to be said again—we read so that we can understand, and if we want to read rapidly then we have to learn to understand rapidly. Consequently the development of efficient reading techniques must be more concerned with the attitudes and purposes of the reader than with the movements of his eyes.

This, of course, does not mean that we can learn to read efficiently by ignoring the visual processes. We have to learn to understand quickly, but we have to learn how to take in more than we are perhaps accustomed to take in at a single glance. The two processes are however connected. If we can learn to understand more quickly what we read, then that in itself will help us to widen our recognition span, i.e. to take in more words at a single glance.

The interpretation and reaction which takes place when we read depend on certain interacting processes. Primarily they depend on the sharpness of the reader's vision. A person with faulty eyesight is not going to be an efficient reader until he has had his eyes tested and corrected by a competent eye-specialist. They also depend on the reader's ability to deal competently with the ideas contained in the lines of print when they have been transmitted to his brain, and on the speed and accuracy of perception.

None of these processes is of more importance to the would-be efficient reader than any other. They are all necessary and must all function together if we are to read efficiently.

What actually takes place when our eyes focus on a line of print? The movements of the eyes are controlled by muscles which act in co-ordination so that the eyes are pulled side-ways in a series of movements enabling us to read a line of print. As the eyes move along the line of print there are momentary pauses which are called fixations.

If a reader has to focus on each separate word before his eyes can move along to the next word it follows that his reading time can be significantly cut and fatigue lessened if he can learn to take in a whole group of words at a glance. In other words, if he can learn to read phrase by phrase rather than word by word, he will read much more quickly.

The duration of pauses is perhaps not an important difference between a poor reader and a good reader; the good reader reads faster because he makes *fewer* pauses.

The number of words that a reader can take in at a glance is called his recognition span. A child who is taught to read by progressing from letters to syllables and from syllables to words has in the beginning a narrow recognition span. If no attempt is made to widen this recognition span or if necessity does not provide such a child with the opportunity for practice in increasing his reading efficiency he will probably remain a word-by-word reader.

The improvement of reading ability must therefore depend in part on the development of characteristics which are primarily concerned with the actual visual processes. This involves the development of as wide a recognition span as possible with a consequent reduction of the number of pauses per line. It involves also a speeding up of the pauses and a reduction in the number of regressions. In fact, the eye movements of a good reader can be distinguished from the eye movements of a poor reader by their rhythmical movements, the infrequency of regressions, the small number of fixations per line and the brief return sweep to the next line. Whether formal visual exercises can train a reader's eye movements, or whether good eye movements result from a correct psychological attitude towards reading, is still a moot point among the experts, but in case any reader can benefit from formal visual exercises these various points will be discussed so that we can understand more clearly what is involved.

When we glance rapidly across the room or out of the window our eyes do not automatically focus on one single object and blot out everything else around it. We see many things at once, some clearly and some not so clearly. Even if we focus on one object, such as one book in a row of several, we can still see the others.

This is because two kinds of vision—macular and peripheral vision—are being used. If in reading a phrase such as this :

We read to understand

the eyes focus on the black spot in the middle of the phrase, macular vision enables the reader to see clearly the word or words in the centre of the phrase and peripheral vision enables him to see, though less clearly, the words at the ends of the phrase.

A very inefficient reader tends to break up a line into separate and isolated words or even syllables. He reads a line of print in this way :

We read for necessity but we read also for pleasure

Each black dot represents one fixation and such a reader therefore focuses 13 times to read the line. A better reader would read the line like this :

• • • • •

We read for necessity but we read also for pleasure

with a consequent reduction in the number of fixations, a widening of the recognition span, a lessening of fatigue and a considerable increase in speed. But apart from this there is another difference which is of the utmost importance. At each fixation, the phrase he reads is more meaningful than the isolated word pictures perceived by the word-by-word reader, and then put together in a meaningful way.

A really efficient reader would probably read the line like this :

• • •

We read for necessity but we read also for pleasure

Words are not of much use until they blend together in a meaningful pattern, and therefore the phrase reader is not only quicker than the word reader, but he is also much more efficient, because the reading of the meaningful phrases obviously gives a much greater degree of comprehension than the necessarily slower perception of isolated words.

Less than 10 per cent of reading time is spent in actual eye movement, but something over 90 per cent is taken up by the pauses. So if we are to improve our reading by attention to the visual processes, we need to concentrate on the pauses rather than on the eye movements. This means that we must be concerned with trying to interpret more accurately and more rapidly the images which the eyes send to the brain, and also with getting more into these images by extending our recognition spans.

In effect, we must be concerned with practice which makes increasing demands on our perceptive capacities, so that as the interpretation of peripheral vision becomes sharper and more efficient, the recognition span will be wider, and more material will be assimilated at each reading pause.

The perception exercises suggested in the next chapter will help many people to cut down the time spent on each pause and to widen the recognition span. The exercises have a psychological, not an organic, effect. They increase the reader's confidence by showing him what he is capable of taking in at a single fixation, and by quickening up his mental responses to the visual images. In other words, their purpose is not to tone up lazy eye muscles but to quicken the understanding.

Most people who want to improve can become very efficient readers without these kinds of exercises. Such exercises are, however, a convenient way of showing readers what they are capable of, and consequently increasing their confidence. To keep this in proportion it is worth repeating that it is far more important to concentrate all your powers of attention on the meaning of a passage and the onward progression of the ideas than to start getting worried about the number of pauses your eyes are making, or the extent of your recognition span.

The speed at which a person can read depends ultimately on what happens in his mind when the message is received from the eyes. Consequently the would-be efficient reader should concern himself much more with the psychological aspects of reading than with the actual eye movement. A person with good eye movements probably has them *because he is an efficient reader*, and it is unlikely that anyone is ever an efficient reader purely because he has good eye movements.

Much of what has been said so far is obvious to anyone who cares to think carefully about the reading process. But many people are still chary of the very idea of speed in reading. It is true to say that in many circumstances rapid reading is considerably more efficient than slow reading. The instruction "read the passage slowly and carefully", so often repeated during school-days, implies that slow reading means careful reading, and perhaps this is one reason why there is still widespread suspicion of rapid reading methods.

The idea that slow reading should be grouped with careful or efficient reading is a fallacy. With many kinds of reading material, rapid reading, provided it is really *reading*, can give a greater degree of comprehension than slow reading for the simple reason that the efficient reader takes in meaningful phrases at each fixation and the slow reader does not. It is also more efficient because the slower the rate of reading the more opportunity the mind has to wander and to think of other things. Rapid reading implies an intense concentration on the meaning of the material and not a vague process of hopeful skimming.

Before we start considering particular perception exercises here is another reading passage. It is taken from Vance Packard's *The Hidden Persuaders* and is concerned with the use of mass psychoanalysis in advertising campaigns. As you read forget about recognition spans and fixations and concentrate only on getting the ideas accurately and quickly from the page without regressing. Look for these ideas deliberately. Be determined to understand what the writer is telling you. When you have read the passage try to reproduce the main ideas in your own words.

There are no questions to help you this time. Remember the comprehension weaknesses you may have experienced when you read the last passage and try to avoid them this time. When you have written your brief summary of the main ideas check them carefully. Always try to find out why omissions and misrepresentations have occurred.

Time the passage and give yourself a comprehension grading as before.

From *The Hidden Persuaders*
by VANCE PACKARD

"The use of mass psychoanalysis to guide campaigns of persuasion has become the basis of a multi-million-dollar industry. Professional persuaders have seized upon it in their groping for more effective ways to sell us their wares— whether products, ideas, attitudes, candidates, goals, or states of mind.

This depth approach to influencing our behaviour is being used in many fields and is employing a variety of ingenious techniques. It is being used most extensively to affect our daily acts of consumption. The sale to us of billions of dollars' worth of United States products is being significantly affected, if not revolutionized, by this approach, which is still only barely out of its infancy. Two-thirds of America's hundred largest advertisers have geared campaigns to this depth approach by using strategies inspired by what marketers call 'motivation analysis'.

Meanwhile, many of the nation's leading public-relations

experts have been indoctrinating themselves in the lore of psychiatry and the social sciences in order to increase their skill at 'engineering' our consent to their propositions. Fund raisers are turning to the depth approach to wring more money from us. A considerable and growing number of our industrial concerns (including some of the largest) are seeking to sift and mould the behaviour of their personnel—particularly their own executives—by using psychiatric and psychological techniques. Finally, this depth approach is showing up nationally in the professional politicians' intensive use of symbol manipulation and reiteration on the voter, who more and more is treated like Pavlov's conditioned dog.

The efforts of the persuaders to probe our everyday habits for hidden meanings are often interesting purely for the flashes of revelation they offer us of ourselves. We are frequently revealed, in their findings, as comical actors in a genial if twitchy Thurberian world. The findings of the depth probers provide startling explanations for many of our daily habits and perversities. It seems that our subconscious can be pretty wild and unruly.

What the probers are looking for, of course, are the *whys* of our behaviour, so that they can more effectively manipulate our habits and choices in their favour. This has led them to probe why we are afraid of banks; why we love those big fat cars; why we really buy homes; why men smoke cigars; why the kind of car we draw reveals the brand of gasoline we buy; why housewives typically fall into a hypnoidal trance when they get into a supermarket; why men are drawn into auto showrooms by convertibles but end up buying sedans; why junior loves cereal that pops, snaps, and crackles.

We move from the genial world of James Thurber into the chilling world of George Orwell and his Big Brother, however, as we explore some of the extreme attempts at probing and manipulating now going on.

Certain of the probers, for example, are systematically feeling out our hidden weaknesses and frailties in the hope that they can more efficiently influence our behaviour. At one of the largest advertising agencies in America psychologists on the staff are probing sample humans in an attempt to find how to identify, and beam messages to, people of high anxiety, body consciousness, hostility, passiveness, and so on. A Chicago advertising agency has been studying the house-wife's menstrual cycle and its psychological concomitants in order to find the appeals that will be more effective in selling her certain food products.

Seemingly, in the probing and manipulating nothing is immune or sacred. The same Chicago ad agency has used psychiatric probing techniques on little girls. Public-relations experts are advising churchmen how they can become more effective manipulators of their congregations. In some cases these persuaders even choose our friends for us, as at a large "community of tomorrow" in Florida. Friends are furnished along with the linen by the management in offering the homes for sale. Everything comes in one big, glossy package.

Sombre examples of the new persuaders in action are appearing not only in merchandising but in politics and industrial relations. The national chairman of a political party indicated his merchandising approach to the election of 1956 by talking of his candidates as products to sell. In many industrial concerns now the administrative personnel are psychoanalysed, and their futures all charted, by trained out-side experts. And then there is the trade school in California that boasts to employers that it socially engineers its graduates so that they are, to use the phrase of an admiring trade journal, 'custom-built men' guaranteed to have the right attitudes from the employer's standpoint.

What the persuaders are trying to do in many cases was well summed up by one of their leaders, the president of the Public Relations Society of America, when he said in an address to members: "The stuff with which we work is the fabric of men's minds." In many of their attempts to work over the fabric of our minds the professional persuaders are receiving direct help and guidance from respected social scientists. Several social-science professors at Columbia Uni-versity, for example, took part in a seminar at the university attended by dozens of New York public-relations experts. In the seminar one professor, in a sort of chalk talk, showed these manipulators precisely the types of mental manipulation they could attempt with most likelihood of success.

All this probing and manipulation has its constructive and

its amusing aspects; but also, I think it fair to say, it has seriously antihumanistic implications. Much of it seems to represent regress rather than progress for man in his long struggle to become a rational and self-guiding being. Something new, in fact, appears to be entering the pattern of American life with the growing power of our persuaders."

CHAPTER 6

Perception Exercises

THERE are many different kinds of perception exercises. Some reading courses use a tachistoscope, a device which flashes digits, words and phrases on to a screen at varying speeds. Such machines have their uses, but their main effect probably lies in stimulating motivation. There is nothing like a piece of expensive machinery for urging people on or persuading them that they are getting their money's worth.

Other courses do the same kind of work without any machinery. The reader uses a piece of card which has cut into it windows corresponding to the length of a normal word, a set of digits or a short phrase. At the bottom of each window there is an arrow which serves as a guide to the centre of the image when it appears in the window. The idea is to pull the appropriate window rapidly over a word, a group of digits or a phrase so that the image is visible in the window for a split second and then covered again.

The exercises are graded so that the reader can progress from one-syllable words to multi-syllable words and then to phrases as his perception becomes sharper and he develops confidence in his ability to differentiate immediately and accurately between similar words.

By speeding up responses such exercises also reduce the tendency some people have to articulate silently—a weakness which limits their speed of reading to their speed of speaking. In addition they help to break the habit of reading word by word because they make the reader aware of his capacity to assimilate word groups. This, in turn, helps towards the ability to read a normal line of print in three or four fixations. Although there are reports of some super-readers who can take in complete lines at a single glance and never need to move their eyes horizontally, for our purposes anyone who can read lines of normal length accurately in three or four fixations is doing very well.

Valuable as they are in certain circumstances, many examples of these exercises must be omitted from this book because of limited space. Instead the reader is recommended to do some perception training by making a card of the type mentioned above and practising on the lists of words and phrases which can be found in most language text-books and vocabulary books. Place the card with a suitably sized window immediately above the first word in the list so that as the card is pulled downwards with a rapid jerk the first word will become visible for a split second and then covered again. A piece of paper should be placed at the right of the card so that when the word or phrase is covered again it can be *written down*. The reader should try as far as possible not to repeat the words or phrases when he reads them. The object is to get as close as possible to an instantaneous response.

Useful perception practice can also be gained by looking quickly at car registration numbers, or the information that appears on the credits at the end of a television programme. A telephone directory can be used for practice in reading digits. Another good exercise is to pick out a key word in a newspaper headline and then, without reading the article, let your eyes travel rapidly down the column, count the number of times the word is used, and then go through the column again and see if any mention of the word has been missed.

To give some idea of the sharpness of your peripheral vision here is a reading pyramid. Fix your eyes at the top of the black line which runs vertically downwards. Do not allow your eyes to move horizontally. Move them vertically down the line at a steady pace so that you are reading each line in one fixation. If you find yourself moving your eyes horizontally, making two or even three fixations to a line, stop reading and make up your mind to keep your eyes firmly fixed on the vertical line.

```
                and now
               they want
              to get away
             from that old
            tradition which
           failed to alter a
          pattern of teaching
         which was essentially
        bound up with that time
       when the grammar of Latin
      and Greek were found to be a
     necessity for learning how to
    use the English language with a
   true sense of decorum and without
  turning it into a mere vulgar noise
```

If you managed to read more than half of that pyramid without any horizontal eye-movements you will find that practising reading the narrower columns of a newspaper will be of value. Try to read the columns by making only two fixations to each line. Draw two thin lines vertically down the column to assist you in keeping the two fixations. The column you select will then look something like this:

```
Authorities differed in the House
of Lords this evening on the
advisability of having a Minister
responsible for the arts. Lord
Cottesloe, chairman of the Arts
Council, thought the suggestion
made recently by a group of M.P.s
a deplorable mistake . . . etc.
```

(The Daily Telegraph)

For a little preliminary practice, here is a short passage taken from a newspaper column of normal width. To enable you to practise reading a newspaper column with two fixations to each line the column has been divided and a vertical line drawn through each half. Read *across* the page taking care to focus only on the vertical lines.

1st Fixation	2nd Fixation
In the early	stages of development
computers were used	only by scientists
and mathematicians	who were
familiar with the	internal construction
of their machines.	As soon as
other people began	to use them
automatic programming	became essential,
and during the past	ten years this
development has been	one of the most
important parts	of computer research.
Broadly speaking,	automatic programming
is concerned with	developing
logically simple and	widely understandable
languages in which	the tasks to be
performed by	a computer
can be specified.	

(*The Guardian*)

On the opposite page is a similar passage broken up in the same way. Concentrate on moving the focus of your eyes from the black line in the first column to the black line in the second. Forget all about speed, concentrate only on a steady progression which will enable you to assimilate the information by making only one fixation for each half of a complete line.

1st *Fixation*	2nd *Fixation*
One would like	to describe Alec
as a plain	blunt man
except that his	bluntness barely
disguised an	exceptional shrewdness
and his plainness	was on
such a vast scale	that every
feature was	accentuated from
the glittering	grey eyes and
enormous jaw to	the solid expanse
of paunch balanced	on elephantine
thighs and huge	flat feet.
Chronic catarrh was	his only weakness.
Like Job's war-horse	that smelt the
battle afar off,	he trumpeted
constantly,	his bulbous nose
clothed in thunder	and a succession
of large white	handkerchieves.
Believing himself	alone in his
affliction he considered	it mockery
for anyone else	even to produce
a handkerchief.	Such was the strength
of his personality	and the might
of his wrath	that most
ordinary mortals	including Directors
of Education	preferred to sniff
in misery	rather than risk
the consequences	of even a
surreptitious wipe.	

(*The Guardian*)

After doing some more practice on newspaper columns try
the following exercise. It is a complete feature article from
The Guardian reproduced so that the reader, by making one
fixation for each line, can see how capable he is of assimilat-

ing information accurately by reading *phrases* (or word groups) instead of words. Do not time this exercise. Concentrate on reading each phrase in one glance only. Do not worry if you think you are missing information. Read progressively, do not regress. At the end of the passage there is a comprehension test.

300 Years of Postal Service

Britain's oldest
State monopoly is
celebrating its
tercentenary by an
issue of
commemorative stamps this
summer. As a form of
public service
the Post Office began
when the Government
found it necessary
to censor
correspondence.
The easiest way of
doing this was to
make the postal services
a Government monopoly
and both Elizabeth I
and James I
took steps to prohibit
the private carrying
of letters.
It was not, however, until
the Act of 1660
for creating and
establishing a Post Office
that stress was laid
on the necessity
for centralised administration.
In effect, the Act
did little more
than legalise Cromwell's
measures of 1657,
but from that day to this
the postal services have been
a nationalised institution.

After the Restoration
the new Postmaster General,
Colonel Henry Bishop,
"farmed" the Post Office
in the same way as
his predecessors had done
except that the value
had increased
to £21,500.
Abuses such as
the franking system—
which enabled
Members of Parliament
and others in
the royal service
to send their mail
free of charge—continued,
but Colonel Bishop,
in a determined effort
to augment his income,
extended the range
and increased the speed
of the service.
In the later years
of the seventeenth century,
when the profits
were used to pay
Court pensions
and Royal mistresses,
the growing reputation
of the Post Office
was almost entirely due
to a series
of efficient
Postmasters General
such as

Colonel Roger Whitley
and Philip Frowde.
The Record Room
of the G.P.O.
still has a collection
of Colonel Whitley's
correspondence
which shows
not only his zeal
but also
his exasperation
with the slackness
of some
of his employees.
"I am credibly informed",
he wrote to one
unfortunate postmistress,
"that your horse tired
at Lechlade last week
and was there
supplied by one
out of a cart.
This is scandalous."
After the 1660 Act
the next great reform
came through
private enterprise.
Emulating
Louis XIV's
one sou local post
in Paris
a London merchant,
William Dockwra, started
the London Penny Post.
He established hundreds
of receiving offices,
hourly collections,
four to eight
deliveries a day
in the greater part
of London
and between
ten and twelve
in the business centres.
As soon as
his enterprise began

to show a profit,
the Duke of York,
on whom
the Post Office revenues
had been settled,
brought a number
of actions
against Dockwra,
who had to pay
£100 damages
for infringing
the Government monopoly.
But the venture
had been so successful
that almost immediately
after the law-suit
the Post Office revived it
as an official service.

In 1711
another important
Post Office Act
was passed
"for establishing
a General Post Office
for all
Her Majesty's Dominions
and for settling
a weekly sum
of the revenues thereof
for the service
of the war . . ."
This act provided
for postal services
to the American
and West Indian colonies
and prohibited
Post Office employees
from "intermeddling
in elections".
The London Penny Post
received parliamentary sanction
and the almost
time-honoured speeds
of 7 m.p.h. in summer
and 5 m.p.h. in winter

were replaced by
an admonition
to convey letters
"with the greatest speed,
security, and conveniency
that may be".

After these measures
the Post Office went
from strength to strength
during the eighteenth century,
at first
under the influence
of Roger Allen's
reforming zeal
and later
when the development
of the main roads
improved the speed
of communication.
This was
the "romantic" period
of the Post Office.
The fast
stage-coaches arrived
and the post boys
with their
shambling horses,
broken-down carts,
and business arrangements
with highwaymen,
disappeared
from the roads.
The sending of mail
by stage-coach
was illegal
but the public's disregard
of the law
is understandable
when the Bath–London
stage-coach time
of seventeen hours
is compared with
the two days taken
by the mail
in 1780.

The introduction
and organisation
of fast mail-coaches
was undertaken by
John Palmer,
a theatre owner
from Bath.
Strongly supported
by William Pitt
his plans
for carrying mail
at an average speed
of 9 m.p.h.
went on apace
and by 1785
the 400 mile journey
from London to Edinburgh
took only 60 hours.
The impressive departure
of the mail from
The Swan with Two Necks
and The Bull and Mouth
became part
of the sights
of London.
The mail-coach era
ended with the construction
of the railways,
and the last
London mail-coach
left for its
final run
in 1845.
The volume of mail
continued to increase
and when Rowland Hill
established
his penny post
in 1840
the previous
year's record
of 82,000,000 letters
was doubled.
The revenue, however,
dropped
to one-third

and it was
not until 1875
when the number
of letters
had increased
by 1,000 per cent.
that the revenue
reached
the 1839 total
of £1,600,000.

The famous
penny blacks
made their appearance
on May 6, 1840,
and 68,000,000
were sold
in the first year,
each sheet carrying
the warning
"in wetting
the back
be careful not
to remove the cement".
The same popularity
was not enjoyed by
William Mulready's
design for stamped
envelopes and covers
and one
contemporary writer
irreverently deflated
the pictorial symbolism
of Britannia
by describing how,
"At her feet
is a lion
wot's taking a nap
And a dish-cover
rests on her
legs and her lap. . . ."
The invention
of the pillar box
was claimed by
both Rowland Hill
and Anthony Trollope.

In 1855
the first one
was erected in London
at the corner of
Fleet Street
and Farringdon Street
and by 1857
they were no longer
a novelty even on
the country roads.
In 1870,
six years after
Rowland Hill's retirement,
the Postmaster General's
report referred to
"changes greater than
any which
had occurred
since the reforms
of 1839".
The growth of the
main postal services
continued,
the Post Office Savings Bank
was inaugurated,
the telegraph system
nationalised,
and halfpenny postcards
were issued
for the first time.
In the 1880's
postal orders
and the parcel post
came into being
and by the close
of the century
rates to the colonies
had been reduced,
an inland letter
weighing four ounces
went for a penny
and letters
were being delivered
by postmen
at every house
in Britain.

Comprehension Test

1. Is the Post Office Britain's second oldest state monopoly?
2. What was the date of the Act of "creating and establishing a Post Office"?
3. What was the system called that enabled members of Parliament and others in the royal service to send their mail free of charge?
4. Did the Post Office show a profit in the later years of the seventeenth century?
5. Who started the London Penny Post?
6. What was the average speed at which the mail travelled before the London Penny Post received parliamentary sanction?
7. When was the "romantic" period of the Post Office?
8. In 1785 how long did the journey from London to Edinburgh take by mail-coach?
9. When Rowland Hill established his penny post in 1840, did the number of letters going through the post double or treble or quadruple?
10. Were the famous Penny Blacks ridiculed at first?
11. Who beside Rowland Hill claimed to have invented the pillar box?
12. By which date were letters being delivered by postmen at every house in Britain?

When you have completed the answers correct them by looking back at the text. If you have made any mistakes remember that the fault may not be due to the fact that you have been trying to take in more words at a glance than you are perhaps accustomed to. Always try to decide why you made a mistake and thus get to know what kind of reading weaknesses you have.

As your peripheral vision gets sharper attempt to read some short news items in the newspaper without moving your eyes horizontally. Read straight down the column. Do not worry about speed with this kind of exercise. When you have done the reading, summarise the main information and then check with the original to see what, if anything, you have missed or misunderstood by reading in this way.

CHAPTER 7

Regression, Vocalisation and Inner Speech

THE inefficient reader slows down his reading and hinders his comprehension when he reads word-by-word or makes an unnecessary number of eye movements to take in a line of print. But if we took a film of the eye movements of an inefficient reader another fault would become evident. We should see that his eye movements are not by any means always progressive, that is, his eyes do not always follow the line of print from left to right and then sweep back to the beginning of the next line. Instead, they dart backwards and forwards, up and down, with occasional rest pauses, in a manner which is increasingly alarming as the standard of reading decreases.

This tendency to look back aimlessly at what has already been read and which therefore should have been understood is called regression. It is a common fault and a serious one. It breaks up the flow of meaning and consequently interferes with the reader's comprehension as well as reducing the rate of reading. It is tiring, uneconomical and often unnecessary. Regression must not, however, be confused with re-reading.

Some people defend regression as sometimes necessary for adequate comprehension. They maintain that to read something twice or even three times helps to fix the facts in their minds, presumably working on the basis that repetition assists retention. But reading something twice is not the same thing as regressing. Re-reading can be done deliberately and for specific purposes. Regression is haphazard. It is a faltering grasshopper activity which has no place in planned, efficient reading.

Material should be read so that the reader understands what the writer is saying. If he does not understand then there is either something wrong with the writing or there is something wrong with the reading. If there is something wrong with the writing—ambiguity, clumsiness, lack of logic, etc.—then some form of re-reading is often necessary. But if the writing is competent, then the efficient reader ought to be able to adjust his speed and techniques in such a way that he can take in at one reading what the writer has to say. If he fails to do this he will start regressing and consequently waste time which he could have saved by reading properly in the first place.

Regression frequently occurs when the reader realises at the end of a line or sentence that he has not grasped the meaning and then makes matters worse by failing to go back methodically to look deliberately for the meaning at the place where the breakdown in understanding occurred. Instead, he allows his eyes to flit around hopefully. Sometimes he succeeds in repairing the breakdown, sometimes he fails. Regression then becomes a habit because the reader does not ask himself why he failed to understand and makes no attempt to isolate the cause.

If we accept that regression is a serious weakness and we wish to reduce or eliminate it we must first try to be clear about what causes it. This is not easy because there are many causes. Sometimes regression is due to an inability to concentrate and in this case the cause of the lack of concentration must be found. Is it because of distractions? If so, either get rid of the distractions or do the reading some other time. There is no point in getting irritated or in merely looking at the lines of print without taking in the meaning.

Or are you a day-dreamer whose day-dreams are invariably conjured up by the connotations of words or different bits of information leading your mind into pleasing by-ways which are completely unconnected with the purpose of the reading?

The way to overcome this is to learn to get involved in what you have to read. Start off by getting yourself in the proper frame of mind. Make quite certain that your purpose in reading is clearly defined. Get the right mental set and then plan your reading according to a particular schedule. If a report of a familiar type which you have to read contains 5,000 words, set aside a definite half hour in which to read it. This means that your average reading speed will be well under 200 words a minute and this should give you ample time. Make sure that you are not going to be disturbed during the half hour you have set aside, and tell yourself that at the end of that time you are going to answer a comprehension test on the report. Then begin your reading in a spirit of firm determination to pick out and assimilate the information you require.

In preparing for determined work of that sort it is important to begin by setting yourself a goal which is easily attainable. Then, if you find that concentration is difficult, you can tell yourself that you only have to concentrate for half an hour, and after that you can let your mind wander if it wants to. When you have learnt to concentrate for half an hour, or even 20 minutes, gradually increase the length of time. But make certain that you really do concentrate during the time you set yourself.

Regression may also be caused by weakness in vocabulary, lack of knowledge of the subject one is reading about, or by reading too quickly. Overcoming faults such as these may not be easy but at least the remedies are obvious.

Frequent regressions can also be due to habit and various psychological factors such as lack of confidence. In many cases the regressive reader looks back over what he has just read to make sure that he has understood something properly and then finds that in fact he understood it in the first place. He has therefore much in common with the kind of man who has to get out of bed to make sure he has locked the back door or who is always unnecessarily checking the time of appointments.

There are probably as many answers to this kind of psychological trouble as there are professional psychologists. But most people would agree that, in general, confidence needs to be restored. Sometimes this can be done effectively by the use of reading films which emphasise the pattern of eye movements by presenting a page of print on the screen in such a way that the words outside the actual phrase being read are out of focus. This forces the reader to progress as each new phrase becomes readable. There is thus no possibility of regression and as the student learns that he is capable of getting the meaning without regressing the habit tends to disappear.

Mechanical assistance of this kind, though helpful, is not by any means necessary. A lot can be done for oneself by setting a series of easily attainable but progressive goals and practising regularly. In general, anyone who is worried by regression can help himself in several ways. First, when he becomes aware that he is regressing he must always ask himself why, and if he can isolate the cause, take steps to remedy it. Second, he must always concentrate on getting the meaning and make a conscious effort at onward progression, resisting any tendency to go back. Third, he must always carefully define the purpose of each piece of reading he undertakes, and practise adjusting his reading rate to the difficulty of the material.

In short, regression is not much of a problem to the reader who tackles each piece of reading in a determined manner intent on finding the meaning and progressing from one idea to the next. The tendency to regress through lack of confidence is almost always, in ordinary reading, connected with a lack of faith in the value of constant progression. The reader who regresses must discover *for himself* that if he keeps going the meaning will frequently become clear and therefore most regressions are unnecessary.

Vocalisation

When a child is taught to read he learns by reading aloud. He recognises the shapes of words and learns to identify those shapes with particular sounds and meanings. Right at the beginning the pronunciation of the words is of great importance and the unit of pronunciation is the word or even syllable. At this stage the child is involved with the mechanics of reading. As he reads aloud slowly and hesitantly the number of fixations he makes for each line approximates to the number of words. If one or two long words appear he breaks them up into syllables.

When the child is capable of getting meaning from the page in this way he is allowed to read by himself. At first he often continues to read aloud because the actual sound of the word is at this stage essential for its meaning. Gradually the sound he makes as he reads dies down, at first to a mutter and then to a mere mouthing of the words. From then on his efficiency as a reader depends on a great many factors but only rarely is he given any further instruction in *how* to read. In most schools, even today, reading instruction does not go very far beyond the mere mechanics of reading.

This is not a criticism of teachers but a criticism of an educational system which allows classes to be too large for any sort of regular individual attention and which has made such a fetish of examinations that the "spoon-feeding" of information has in many cases become a substitute for the pupil getting, under guidance, his own information from books. It is an extreme view that states that the formal lecture should have become obsolescent with the invention of the printing press, but teaching young people to get information from books accurately and rapidly does not appear to be a feature of our educational system to which much attention is paid.

One result of this is that many people find reading a wearisome chore *because they are poor readers*. And many of them are poor readers because their reading instruction ceased at a time when it was necessary for them to pronounce the words before getting the meaning. This means that the reading speed of such a person is tied to his rate of pronunciation which is painfully and unnecessarily slow.

It is not just the speed of the reading which is affected when the number of fixations per line equals the number of words or even syllables. The comprehension of such a reader is also frequently poor because he is much too involved with the mechanics of reading. Everyone who is conscious of muttering words to himself or of being aware of the sound of words as he reads must get it firmly into his head that words do not have to be pronounced before they can be understood. In addition, reading aloud is obviously more tiring than completely silent reading because of the muscular activity involved.

Anyone who, as an adult, still makes unnecessary *movements* of the tongue or lips is unlikely to make much progress in reading efficiently until both sound and movement have been eliminated. Sometimes merely knowing about the habit does the trick. But when the fault has been a long established habit its removal can be difficult. Some suggested remedies are to read with a hand over the mouth, to put a pipe or a pencil between the teeth, or to chew gum. In fact almost any means of keeping the mouth, tongue and vocal chords still will suffice until the reader has learnt to read without their assistance.

Among literate adults actual reading aloud so that it is audible is not very common, but reading "silently aloud" is a weakness from which a great many people suffer. Everyone, of course, actually speaks or at least mutters words aloud when they learn to read, but usually the sound is reduced or eliminated as normal reading progress is made. The reader who is merely aware of the sound of words as he reads is not nearly so hampered as the person in whom movement or sound can be detected. In fact, most people experience some measure of "inner speech" as it is called. However, the more it can be reduced the better. The main reasons for this reduction and eventual elimination or near elimination are, firstly, that significant improvements in speed are not possible until the reader is capable of breaking this sound-barrier and reading at a speed that is faster than his speed of speaking. Secondly, it can be shown that a noticeable amount of inner-speech definitely hinders comprehension. The first point is self-evident, the second can easily be proved if the reader selects a difficult passage, reads it aloud and then considers how much of it he has understood. In almost all cases he will find that the reading will be slow and the comprehension poor because at least part of his mental activity has been devoted to problems of pronunciation and there is too much consciousness of self and too little consciousness of the writer's meaning.

Does the elimination of inner speech mean that a poem or a piece of writing that depends for its effect on the sound of carefully chosen words cannot be appreciated? It certainly does not mean that. The efficient reader adapts his speed, methods and techniques to the purpose for which he is reading. Some material he can dispose of at thousands of words a minute, other material might need to be read slowly and with frequent re-reading to obtain its full flavour, with other material the reader might *want* to hear the sound of the words.

Generally speaking, the main remedy for "inner speech" rests on whether or not the reader can grasp and put into practice the fact that efficient reading must be much more concerned with the ideas for which the words are symbols than with the actual words themselves. Any undue measure of vocalisation or inner speech must mean that the reader suffers from an inability to read for ideas. The main remedy then does not depend on biting pencils or chewing gum but on developing a much more positive approach to reading and learning to read for ideas, for meaning rather than for words. The poor reader who makes a sustained effort to do this will find a gradual reduction in his awareness of inner speech as his response to the *meaning* of words becomes less consciously dependent on their sound. He will also find that the tendency to regress gradually disappears.

CHAPTER 8

Readability

WE read at different speeds largely because our purposes in reading vary to some extent every time we read something new. But other factors affect our reading speeds, and one of the most obvious is the way in which the material is presented. Reading material varies in difficulty partly because of its subject matter, and partly because of the way in which it is presented. "Readability" is a convenient word to describe the level of difficulty involved.

In the U.S.A., "readability formulas" have been developed for assessing the standard of difficulty of any reading matter. One purpose of these formulas is to help the reader to assess the readability of the material *before* he begins to read, in the hope that he will be able to deal with it more efficiently, particularly if he wishes to work out a reading schedule.

Most of these formulas are based on the belief that difficulty increases as word length and sentence length increase. So, if we are faced with a 10,000 word report and wish to calculate the length of time it would take to read, we can be helped by making a random selection of words and sentences and considering their length. Such methods, however, are no more than rough guides because it is not possible to judge readability against an absolute standard. It is not only the material that has to be assessed but also the reader's capabilities in relation to that material. These capabilities depend largely on the kind of vocabulary with which the reader is familiar, his ability to give, accurately and quickly, meaningful equivalents of obscure passages, and his familiarity with different sentence and paragraph structures.

In other words, the standard of readability is largely a personal matter, and everyone has to decide for himself the ease or difficulty with which he will be able to read a particular passage. Word and sentence length can certainly be a help. If the opening words of a book on Reading were "Reading is a processing skill of symbolic reasoning, sustained by the interfacilitation of an intricate hierarchy of substrata factors that have been mobilised as a psychological working system, and pressed into service in accordance with the purpose of the reader . . . etc." and if the random selection of words and phrases showed us that words and sentences of a similar length were used throughout the book, we could assume that the introductory sentence was perhaps typical of many of the sentences we would have to read if we tackled the whole book.

The average length of words and sentences, the kind of vocabulary and the structure of the paragraphs are guides to the readability of a book or passage, but too much importance must not be attached to them. Consider for instance these sentences:

I am that I am.

A poem should contain within itself the reason why it is so and not otherwise.

Hippopotamuses are quadrupeds inhabiting African rivers.

Accurate examination must invariably precede accurate diagnosis, and accurate diagnosis will always remain indispensable to successful treatment.

If we were asked which two sentences are easiest to understand most of us would choose the last two. Yet the third sentence is longer and contains longer words than the first, and the same applies if we compare the fourth sentence with the second.

Because of the limitations of readability formulas and because levels of readability change frequently even within chapters, it is far better for the reader to concentrate on improving his ability to adjust his reading techniques rapidly and confidently to suit any level of readability.

This is easier said than done, but a great deal of help

can be gained by learning something of the *writer's* problems. Communication, whether in speech or in writing, must always be a two-way affair. There is no point in speaking unless someone is going to listen, and there is no point in writing unless someone is going to read what you have written. In a sense, reading is the reverse of writing. Reading and writing cannot be regarded as two separate and distinct functions because they are both essential parts of the process of communication in which both the sender and the receiver have common problems. If we can recognize and appreciate the writer's problems and the methods he uses to overcome them it will help to make the reading easier by increasing both comprehension and speed in adapting reading techniques to different kinds of writing.

A lot of people go to a lot of trouble to make reading easier for us. Look at a page of a newspaper and consider all the devices which writers, editors and printers use for the purpose of communicating news and opinions to the reader.

Headlines are there to help us select at a glance what we want to read and what we can omit. The sub-headings help us through the articles by picking out particular points of interest for each section. A brief glance at these can give us a definite mental set for our reading and help us to get involved in the process of extracting the information quickly and accurately. In the same way a book or a report will often have chapter or section headings and frequently headings within the chapters or sections. Their purpose is the same. They are there to assist us. And, as readers, it is our job to make full use of that assistance.

Information presented to us in print is not slung down haphazardly but written according to a definite plan. The object of this planning is to ensure as far as possible that the reader will be able to understand the information accurately and quickly. It follows then that if we can make ourselves aware of the ways in which the information has been presented, in other words, get our thoughts in line with those of the writer, we shall stand a better chance of assimilating the information.

Apart from selecting the right kinds of words, the writer

attempts to organise his material in the sequence in which it can most easily be understood. To do this he is concerned largely with the structure of sentences and paragraphs, the two principal vehicles for communicating information in a meaningful way.

A sentence is a group of words which has meaning, a complete thought unit. But if these thought units are just strung together with only full-stops dividing one thought from another, the reader is going to find considerable difficulty in discovering what the writer wishes to emphasise. Consequently, if the reader cannot determine which ideas the writer wishes to emphasise, reading for meaning will be extremely difficult.

To overcome this difficulty the writer groups his sentences into paragraphs. An understanding and a familiarity with the construction of paragraphs is one of the marks of the efficient reader because paragraphs exist for the sole purpose of making the reading easier. And the readability of any piece of writing depends to a great extent on the writer's skilful use of paragraphs.

Here is a paragraph taken from the *Penguin Science Survey, 1961*. It is by Dr. M. J. Wells and is the first paragraph of an article called "The Brain of the Octopus".

"Almost all animals have nerve cells with very similar properties. The individual nerve units from a lobster, a snail, or a man all conduct messages in the form of electrical pulses, which travel along them apparently as a result of the same physico-chemical processes. The impulses in any one nerve fibre do not vary in amplitude or speed of transmission, but they can within limits vary in frequency, so that information is always conveyed in terms of variation in the number and frequency of pulses. Individual cells may vary in speed of transmission of pulses, but they are otherwise fundamentally alike. This functional similarity is to a considerable extent reflected in structure. Nerve cells from different animals look so much alike under the microscope that we generally cannot identify the species or even the major group of animals from which any given sample is taken."

This paragraph contains five sentences and therefore at least five pieces of information. The very fact that the writer has presented the facts in one paragraph means two things. First, that all the facts are related in some way. Second, that they are put together for a particular purpose.

These two points ought to be self-evident. If the facts were unrelated they would not be grouped together in one paragraph; and they must have been put together for a particular purpose, otherwise there would not be any point in writing the paragraph. The relationship between the various sentences —the point they all have in common—is obviously the central theme of the paragraph. Every paragraph should have this central theme either stated in general terms in one sentence and reinforced by the other sentences, or implied when all the sentences are taken together.

The efficient reader must be able to pick out this central theme straight away, otherwise he will not be able to differentiate between main ideas and subordinate ideas.

When the main theme of a paragraph is stated in a sentence that sentence is usually referred to as a topic sentence. Sometimes such a sentence is easy to pick out, sometimes it is more difficult. If there is any difficulty, a reasonably reliable method is to ask "Which is the most important word or phrase in the paragraph?" and then to pick out the sentence which makes the most generalised statement about it.

Even a cursory glimpse at the extract on page 77 will show that the phrase "nerve cells" is absolutely vital to its meaning. In fact, either the complete phrase or the word "nerve" appears in all but one sentence, and the first sentence— "Almost all animals have nerve cells with very similar properties"—makes the most generalised statement about nerve cells. Although the other sentences give important information, in each case the information is a reinforcing detail of the first sentence, the topic sentence, and the generalised meaning of each of the remaining sentences is found in the topic sentence.

But what if the paragraph does not conform to this somewhat idealised picture? What if it is an abnormal or a badly constructed paragraph, or has two or more sentences of equal importance? No hard and fast rule can be given here except to say, possibly unhelpfully, that if you have learned to read for meaning you will soon be able to detect a paragraph in which no single dominating idea is actually stated, and then for the purpose of assimilating and remembering the author's meaning you supply one yourself.

Two examples might be useful here. The first is a very short one :

"The efficient reader does not tire easily; the poor reader does. The efficient reader enjoys reading; the poor reader finds it a chore. The efficient reader always reads with a specific purpose in mind; the poor reader rarely does so."

If we look for a topic word we find that it is "reader". But two sorts of reader are mentioned—the efficient reader and the poor reader. Is one given more prominence than the other or is any one of the three sentences more important than the other? The answer here is "no" because the paragraph is concerned with listing the differences between the efficient reader and the poor reader. Whether we give equal weight to all three sentences or try to summarise them into a generalised statement depends on our purpose in reading. If we are only looking for very general ideas and not details we could construct a topic sentence for ourselves such as : "There are various noticeable differences between the efficient reader and the poor reader."

Similarly there is the kind of paragraph which is sometimes referred to as a "transitional" paragraph and is used to form a bridge between two topics. Such a paragraph might summarise briefly what has gone before and then introduce what is to follow. We cannot say that the summary of what has gone before is more important than the introduction to what follows. We merely recognise the paragraph for what it is—a signpost that tells us where we have been and where we are going.

Another kind of paragraph which does not have a topic sentence is the paragraph which gives instructions.

"When everything is ready and the time of development has been decided, pour the developer into the central hole in the tank lid (the quantity varies according to the size of the film), note the time and insert the agitating spindle and turn intermittently at frequent intervals for the specified time of development. Pour out the developer, fill the tank with clean water and rinse for one minute; empty again and then pour in the hypo (fixing solution) and agitate for a further ten minutes."

The paragraph consists of a sequence of instructions divided into two sentences which tell the reader how to develop a film. The reader does not want any generalised statement. His purpose in reading the paragraph must be to find out how to develop a film and so for him the series of step-by-step instructions cannot be divided into important and less important parts. If the film is to be properly developed all the instructions are of importance.

The matter of topic sentences does not therefore arise in these kinds of writing, and a reader using a book which consists largely of step by step instructions is not usually concerned with prolonged reading. The test of such instructions is whether the reader can follow them easily and exactly.

The efficient writer aims to help the reader to pick out the main stream of his thought by organising these thoughts into groups (paragraphs) each of which has its main or topic sentence, or a single dominant idea. The ability to pick out these topic sentences (or topic ideas) is of inestimable value to the reader for whatever purpose he is reading. If he wishes only to get a general idea of the subject about which he is reading then he may need to read only the topic sentences, and when he has finished the book he will have achieved his object.

On the other hand, if intensive reading is required, he must also pick out the various facts contained in the subsidiary sentences. This does not mean that if he is reading intensively the importance of the topic sentence is lessened. The topic sentence remains of extreme importance because it is a focal point which assists the reader to assimilate the other details by giving them a context and thus making them more meaningful. In learning to read effectively we must think always in terms of meaning. To get the meaning is the object of all reading, and that which is meaningful is more easily remembered.

Merely knowing what a topic sentence is and how it may be found is insufficient in itself to improve reading. Practice is necessary. This practice need not necessarily be formal, it can be done whenever you read a book or magazine. Picking out the topic sentence involves always looking for the main idea. This means that the reader must always ask himself what the writer is getting at and he must read for meaning and follow the writer's line of thought by always keeping the general theme in the foreground. These main ideas are generally found in the topic sentences of the paragraphs.

Leaving aside complexities of subject matter and vocabulary it is fair to say that the more trouble a writer takes over the presentation of his paragraph, that is in organising his subsidiary thoughts around his main thoughts, the higher will be the level of readability. And the more adept the reader is at picking out the topic sentences and the key words, the more his skill in reading will increase the readability of the material. Eventually this ability will become a habit and will operate unconsciously.

The process of communication does not of course finish there. The writer does not present his work just as a series of little groups of satellite ideas revolving neatly round their centres. Nor is the reader only concerned with picking out principal ideas and noting the subsidiary ideas which cling to them. The writer must also be concerned with the connection between his principal ideas so that eventually they become a meaningful whole. Consequently the reader must also be concerned with the means of connection because it is in this way that his reading becomes progressive and accumulative.

To do this important work of connecting his ideas the writer must use particular words and phrases which link together in different ways the ideas he has to put forward. The efficient reader must learn to pick out these words instantaneously and to know what to expect in the sentences that follow.

Such words are sometimes called "link words", although they are also, in their own way, key words. This is because they are words which unlock doors so that we can pass through, words which enable us to progress as we read. Reading after all is a journey of discovery. We start off along a corridor, there are signposts to show us the way, but occasionally we turn off into little blind alleys or retrace our steps to make certain we are going in the right direction. Or we are suddenly beset with doubt about what the last sign said and back we go to check on it. Along the corridor are many doors each one opening on to something new. But the keys are all in different places. After a time we do not have to stop and take the door to bits to get through or search every inch of its surface. We find instead that we have learned to find the key without deliberately thinking about it, and by looking at it we know what we are likely to find in the next room.

What are these link words? Generally speaking they are of three different kinds. *Progressing words* such as "and", "also", "besides", "in addition", tell us that we are going to be given more of the same kind of information as before. *Clarifying words* such as "because", "for example", etc., emphasise or clarify a point by giving a reason or an example. Finally there are *Qualifying words*, such as "but", "although", "not". These make us pause momentarily because the previous statement needs some sort of qualification.

The efficient reader is always on the lookout for such words. In their context he will know immediately what kind of thing to expect. He will think with the author and become used to the way the author uses such words. As he becomes involved in the reading his appreciation of these important words will become largely automatic.

Most of the link words mentioned above are correctly used with particular punctuation marks, and it is safe to say that the more readable a writer's work the more care he takes over punctuation. In the same way the more efficient the reader the more he is aware of punctuation marks because he knows that they are there for the purpose of clarifying the writer's meaning.

As soon as we begin to consider sentence structure in relation to punctuation and link words, it should become obvious that a thorough knowledge of grammatical structure is also an essential part of the equipment of an efficient reader. Apart from the very simple ones, most sentences consist of two kinds of material, some of which is of primary importance and some of which is of secondary importance. The efficient reader is concerned with grasping what is of primary importance to the central theme of whatever he is reading and allowing the subordinate details to fit in where applicable. Such a reader must be able to see immediately where the writer's primary emphasis lies and where his secondary emphasis lies.

We began this chapter by discussing readability, which is often taken to depend on the length of words and of sentences. Although these factors may give a rough guide, others are involved of which grammar and punctuation are of great importance. The writer who observes the rules of grammar and so structures his sentences that the meaning unfolds itself according to particular rules is usually the writer whose work is most readable. But if the reader cannot, through ignorance, benefit from the careful way in which the information has been presented, then he has only himself to blame.

We need always to remember that communication cannot be carried on in a void. At least two people are needed—a speaker and a listener, a writer and a reader. And for communication to be effective there must be competence on both sides. Unfortunately, the listening and reading aspects do not always receive their fair share of attention. They are rarely treated as skills which can be learned in the same way that other skills can be learned. At school we are taught grammar and syntax, how to write a paragraph and connect it to other paragraphs, but we are not always shown how this knowledge can be used to make the reading process considerably more efficient.

CHAPTER 9

Vocabulary

AN efficient reader concentrates on word groups rather than on individual words, but his understanding of written material must depend basically on his knowledge of individual words. The rapid and accurate recognition and interpretation of a wide variety of words are therefore a first necessity for reading improvement because rapid reading of any kind is obviously an impossibility if the reader has to pause constantly to puzzle out the meaning of words.

Apart from its obvious value in reading, writing and speaking, a wide vocabulary is important for *thinking*. In this book a good many phrases containing the word "think" or variations of it have been used—"getting the *thought* off the page", "*thinking* with the author", "finding the pattern of *thought*", etc. Thinking is very hard work. Thomas Edison said, "There is nothing a man will not do in order to avoid the labour of thinking." There is a great deal of truth in the remark, and one of the reasons why people avoid thinking is poor vocabulary. Words are the tools of accurate thought and so, as well as having a good recognition vocabulary, the efficient reader must also be able to *use* a wide variety of words not only in writing and speaking but also in thinking.

The point that needs to be stressed here is that a mere acquaintance with a lot of different words is not sufficient for efficient reading. What is needed is a complete *familiarity* with the meanings and uses of a wide variety of words. The main reason for this is that the more familiar a reader is with the meanings of individual words the less conscious he will be of the actual words themselves, and the more rapidly and accurately he will react to the *whole* meanings of word groups whether they are short phrases or complete paragraphs.

Here is a short list of words chosen from a single issue of
the *Daily Telegraph*.

brochure	infamy
circumspection	indigenous
curriculum	intransigence
chauvinistic	linguistic
corruption	moratorium
cynically	plutocracy
discreet	superficial
exploits (noun)	tardily
excessive	vindication
exacted	verification
forbears	

Most of the words ought to be familiar to a person whose
standard of education is such that he reads *The Times*, the
The Guardian or the *Daily Telegraph* in preference to the
Daily Mirror or the *Daily Sketch*. Look at the words carefully and then consider how many of them you can define
immediately and accurately and how many you would actually use in writing or in conversation.

The rest of this chapter is largely concerned with the needs
of anyone who cannot confidently answer "most of them" to
both questions.

If you now study the words as they are used in their contexts they will seem more familiar, but in some cases the
meanings might still be elusive and many readers will pause
momentarily at several of the words because of some uncertainty about their meanings. Here are the sentences in
which the words occur :

Cromwell's *infamy* and *exploits* seemed to occupy more
time in the school *curriculum* than was necessary.

Many American writers are trying to stem the tide of
linguistic corruption.

On the strength of Haushofen's *superficial* briefing Hess
flew to Britain. The *plutocracy, indigenous* or not, failed to
help him.

If the Russians continue to behave with *discreet circumspection*—certainly it is a big "if"—this in itself will be a most powerful *vindication* of President Kennedy's decision.

What the Secretary General has proposed is a sort of *moratorium*.

Tardily, under pressure, and without *excessive* grace, the British Government has consented to make a grant of £50,000 to Polish ex-Servicemen who are in need.

They are grateful to him for four years of stability and prosperity and their *chauvinistic* pride has been aroused by his policy of "grandeur" and international *intransigence*.

He made it perfectly clear that the emphasis on *verification* will apply throughout.

Nowadays when, perhaps, *cynically*, most of us expect a "free book" to amount to little more than a *brochure* it is pleasant to come across one which has 200 large pages. . . .

Their descendants have *exacted* vengeance for the sufferings their *forbears* endured.

Reading through these sentences after considering the words when isolated from their contexts should bring out three obvious but important facts. First, that our recognition vocabulary is greater than the vocabulary we actually use. Second, that words are easier to interpret when they are in context (i.e. when they are part of a word group). Third, that reading slows down when unfamiliar words appear.

The first recommendation that may be made to anyone who wishes to improve his reading efficiency and is aware of weaknesses in vocabulary is "Be word conscious". This means considerably more than merely looking up unknown words in a dictionary. It means not only being on the alert for new words, but also deliberately putting ourselves into a position where we are likely to encounter new words. It means also that we must be constantly thinking *about* words and using as wide a variety as possible.

The following suggestions about how this can best be accomplished should be used with a certain amount of flexibility. They are not intended to be a rigid formula.

In the first place it is necessary to identify the words we do not know. This is usually a fairly simple matter as the reader either slows down because he realises the meaning is being lost or he stops altogether. When this occurs it is better *not* to look up the word immediately, but to mark it in the margin or to underline it, continue to the end of the chapter or passage, and then return. In many cases, further reading will help to explain the new word, but even if its meaning becomes absolutely clear, it is worth while in the long run to spend a little time on the word that has caused the hesitation.

On returning to the word, try to puzzle out its meaning from the context. Do not look it up in the dictionary straight away. As a simple example let us say that we are baffled by the word "verification" in the sentence quoted above—"He made it perfectly clear that the emphasis on *verification* will apply throughout." The sentence is taken from a parliamentary report during the 1962 Cuba crisis. The context in which the sentence appeared is as follows :

"Mr. Macmillan's mention of the possibility of moving into a wider field of negotiation was noted with approval on both sides of the House. But he made it perfectly clear that the emphasis on verification will apply throughout. In other words, the principle of admitting independent observers will have to be conceded by Russia in any agreement on nuclear tests or general disarmament."

In this context, verification must have quite a lot to do with admitting independent observers. Admitting them for what purpose? Independent observers are usually used for establishing the truth about something and presumably that is what the word means here.

After working out what we think is the meaning we turn to the dictionary. We look up the meaning and find, in this case, that our assumption is correct. The fact that we have first worked out the meaning will help to establish it firmly in our minds. Our ability to remember is very often in direct proportion to the amount of work that has gone into getting the answer. A *quick* look in a dictionary frequently means that the word will have to be looked up several times before its meaning is remembered.

The second stage in the process of becoming word-conscious is to use the dictionary properly. We have checked the meaning of "verification", but if we do not reinforce our knowledge of the word it will not stay with us for long. So first of all we take a good look at the word, noting its spelling and pronunciation. Are we sure that we can use it correctly? Yes, of course we are. We looked up the meaning and found that our assumption was correct. We have *verified* its meaning. But "verify" is not the actual word we looked up so therefore we have learned two words for the price of one.

Is there anything else we can do whilst we have the dictionary open at the appropriate place? Here is the complete entry as it appears in the *Concise Oxford Dictionary* :

> **verify,** v.t. Establish the truth of, examine for this purpose, as *must v. the statement, his figures, am now verifying the items*; (of event, action &c.) bear out, make good, fulfil, (prediction, promise); (Law) append affidavit to (pleadings), support (statement) by proofs. Hence or cogn. verifiability, verification, verifier, nn., verifiable a. [f. OF *verifier* f. med. L *verificare* (*versus* true, see -fy)].

Anyone who does not know what these abbreviations mean will find a full account at the beginning of any reliable dictionary such as the Oxford Dictionary or Chambers's Dictionary.

Our particular interest here is to find out how much can be learned and should be learned from the verification of a single word in a dictionary.

First there are the similar words from the same root: verify, verifiability, verification, verifier, verifiable. Second, there are the different ways in which these words can be used in different contexts. Third, there are the synonyms and words with a similar meaning. Fourth, there is the correct pronunciation of the word. Fifth, there are the details of its etymology.

Consider this last point. Even a limited knowledge of Latin gives a person a flying start when it comes to a rapid working out of the meaning of a long and unfamiliar word. But it is by no means essential to know Latin as a language. What we are primarily interested in here is the way Latin words have been absorbed into the English language. Take, for instance, the word "verify". The student of Latin will know immediately that the English word comes from the Latin *versus* meaning true, and the suffix -fy comes from the Latin *ficare* or *facere* meaning make or produce.

Many of the longer English words can be broken up into their components and the meaning worked out from a very limited knowledge of Latin and Greek words. For instance, "dissatisfaction" falls into three parts

> dis—the prefix
> satis—the root word
> faction—the suffix

The complete word comes directly from the Latin.

dis   means apart, not, the opposite of
satis means enough
fact   comes from the Latin "facere" (to make or do)
ion   is the common suffix forming nouns of quality, state
       or condition.

These prefixes and suffixes occur over and over again in English and many thousands of words are affected. It follows, therefore, that even if we have "little Latin and less Greek" we can make immediate improvements in vocabulary by learning the prefixes, roots and suffixes which come from Latin and Greek.

In fact, a few hours spent in learning the commonest Latin and Greek roots and prefixes can give as much assistance to the reader who wishes to improve his English vocabulary as many hundreds of hours spent in studying Latin and Greek as languages. This does not mean that there is little purpose in learning Latin and Greek. The point is that, if the object of learning Latin and Greek is *only* to improve one's vocabulary, the same benefit can be gained much more easily and quickly by learning a basic list of roots, prefixes and suffixes and adding to this list when new words are learned.

If the reader is unconvinced of the value of learning such a list, let him try to give the meaning of the following words :

amphitheatre, animadversion, antecedent, autonomy, belli-cose, chronology, circumlocution, decalogue, dermatology, empathy, extramural, heliography, heterodox, heptagon, hypercritical, morphology, millepede, omnifarious, om-niscient, ovoid, pentameter, supernumerary, synoptic, vice-roy.

Anyone who experienced difficulty with more than five of the words in the above list would be well advised to study the following lists carefully and regularly.

Prefixes, Suffixes and Roots

The following lists are selections of prefixes, suffixes and roots, mostly from Latin and Greek but including other sources. Studying these lists is not a substitute for using a dictionary. Readers without a knowledge of Latin and Greek will benefit considerably from devoting regular periods of about 10 or 15 minutes to learning the lists, adding to them and studying words other than the examples given.

The Commonest Prefixes

The following fifteen different prefixes are used in over three-quarters of the words which have prefixes. Readers with weak vocabularies are advised to look each one up in a dictionary and study the various ways in which they are used :

ab- (from)

ad- (to)

be- (by)

com- (with)

de- (from)

dis- (apart, not)

en- (in)

ex- (out)

in- (into)

in- or im- (not)

pre- (before)

pro- (in front of, in favour of)

re- (again, back)

sub- (under)

un- (not)

Prefixes

mostly from Latin and Greek, but including other sources

a-	without, not	amorphous
a-, ab-	away, from, off, apart	absent
ad-	to, toward	advent
amb-, amphi-	around, both	amphitheatre, ambiguous
ante-	before	antenatal
anti-	against	antidote
arch-	chief, most important	archbishop, archcriminal
auto-	self	automatic
be-	about	beset, beguile
bene-	well, good	benefactor
bi-	two	biennial
circum-	around	circumference
com-, con-	with, together	companion, congregate
co-, col-		co-operate, collect
contra-	against	contradict
de-	down, completely, from	depend, denude, decentralise
deca-	ten	decade
dia-	through	diameter
dis-	not, opposite of	dislike
duo-	two	dual, duologue
e-, ex-	out of	exhale
extra-	beyond, outside	extramural
hemi-	half	hemisphere
hepta-	seven	heptachord
hexa-	six	hexagon
hyper-	above, excessive	hypercritical
in-	into	instil
in-, im-	not	insecure (note assimilations, e.g. illegal, irreverent)
inter-	between, among	interrupt, intermarriage
intra-, intro-	inside, within	intramural, introvert
iso-	equal, same	isosceles
mal-	bad, wrong	malformed

mis-	wrongly	mislead
mono-	alone, single	monotonous
multi-	many	multipurpose
ob-	in the way of	obstruct
octa-, octo-	eight	octahedron
penta-	five	pentagon
per-	through	perennial
peri-	around	perimeter
poly-	many	polygamy
post-	after	postscript
pre-	before	prehistoric
prime-, primo-	first	primordial, prime-minister
pro-	in front of, favouring	prologue, pro-British
quadri-	four	quadruped
re-	again, back	reappear
retro-	backward	retrograde
semi-	half	semitone
sub-	under	subterranean
super-	above, over	superfluous
syn-, sym-	together	synchronise, sympathy
ter-	three times	tercentenary
tetra-	four	tetrahedron
trans-	across	translate, trans-Atlantic
tri-	three	tripartite
un-	not	unable
uni-	one	unicellular
vice-	in place of	viceroy

Roots

Latin and Greek

aer	air	aerate
amare, amat-	love	amorous, amateur
annus	year	annual
audire, audit-	hear	auditorium
bio	life	biography
capere, capt-	take	captive
caput, capitis	head	capital
chrono	time	chronology

cor, cordis	heart	cordial
corpus, corporis	body	corporation
deus	god	deify
dicere, dict-	say, speak	dictate
ducere, duct-	lead	aqueduct
ego	I	egotism
equi	equal	equidistant
facere, fact-	make, do	manufacture
frater	brother	fraternity
geo	earth	geology
graph	write	calligraphy
homo	alike	homogeneous
locus	place	location
loqui, locut-	speak	eloquence, circumlocution
lux, lucis	light	elucidate
manus	hand	manuscript
mittere, miss-	send	admit, permission
mors, mortis	death	immortal
omni	all	omnipotent
pater, patris	father	paternal
patho	suffering, feeling	sympathy, pathology
pes, pedis	foot	impede, millepede
photo	light	photography
phobia, phobe	fear	hydrophobe, xenophobia
pneum	air, breath, spirit	pneumatic, pneumonia
pono, posit-	place	deposit
potior, posse, potens	be able	potential, possible
quaerere, quaesit-	ask, question, seek	inquiry, query
rogare, rogat-	ask	interrogate
scribere, script-	write	scribble, script
sentire, sens-	feel	sensitive
solus	alone	soloist
soph	wise	sophist, philosopher
spicere, spect-	look	introspective, inspect
spirare, spirat-	breathe	inspiration
tele	far	telegraph
thermos	warm	thermometer
tendere, tens-	stretch	extend
tenere, tent-	hold	tenant

utilis	useful	utility
venire, vent-	come, arrive	convene, advent
vertere, vers-	turn	revert, adverse
videre, vis-	see	supervisor, vision

Suffixes

mostly Latin and Greek, but including other sources

-able, -ible	capable of, fit for	durable, comprehensible
-acy	state or quality of	supremacy
-age	action or state of, belonging to	breakage, bondage, orphanage
-al	relating to	abdominal
-ance, -ence	quality or action of	insurance, corpulence
-ant	forming adjectives of quality; or nouns signifying a personal agent or something producing an effect	defiant, servant, irritant
-arium, -orium	place for	aquarium, auditorium
-ary	place for, dealing with	seminary, dictionary
-ate	cause to be, office of	animate, magistrate
-ation, -ition	action or state of	condition, dilapidation
-cle, -icle	diminutive	corpuscle, icicle
-ferous	producing	coniferous
-ful	full of	colourful
-fy, -ify	make	satisfy, fortify
-hood	state or condition of	childhood
-ic	relating to	historic
-ion	condition or action of	persuasion
-ism	quality or doctrine of	socialism
-itis	inflammation of (medical)	bronchitis
-ity, -ety, -ty	quality or state of	loyalty
-ive	nature of	creative
-ize, ise	make, practise, act like	modernize, advertise, bowdlerize

-logy	indicating a branch of knowledge	biology
-ment	act or condition of	resentment
-metry	measure	gasometer, geometry
-mony	resulting condition	testimony
-oid	resembling	ovoid
-or	person who, or thing which	victor, generator
-ose, -ous	full of	bellicose, murderous
-osis	process or condition of	metamorphosis
-tude	quality or degree of	altitude

The points mentioned so far about the process of being word conscious can be summarised like this :

1. Develop an interest in the way words are made and be able to interpret the most common roots and suffixes.
2. Practise defining words which, although fairly familiar, present some uncertainty.
3. Whenever a new or unfamiliar word appears always try to work out its meaning from the context before using a dictionary.
4. Buy a good dictionary and use it properly, i.e. get as much information from it as you can.
5. Make a list of new words you come across. Practise defining them.

The third point perhaps needs more explanation. How can one work out the meaning of a completely new word without reference to a dictionary or glossary? Sometimes the meaning of the word becomes clear from the context as we saw in the list of words taken from the *Daily Telegraph*. But occasionally the reader is not so fortunate and does not get sufficient help from the context.

Here is a passage taken from W. Sluckin's *Mind and Machines* (Pelican). Some of the words are in italics. We are going to assume that the reader does not know the meaning of these words when he first encounters them and that he is still unaware of their meaning after reading the complete passage.

First, read the passage :

From *Minds and Machines*
by w . s l u c k i n

"Thought Processes

The psychology of thinking is a very wide and ill-defined field. A range of subjects : consciousness, attention, *imagery*, *concept* formation, and others, are relevant to it in a greater or lesser measure. Our particular approach, however, is a relatively restricted one. Our programme in this chapter is, first, to discuss certain general characteristics of thought, then to examine some new models of thinking, and finally to consider to what extent and in what sense machines may be said to think.

Unlike learning, thinking cannot easily be looked at from the point of view of the observer of behaviour because there is nothing or very little to observe when other people think. Admittedly, human beings and even animals behave as if they thought, but our understanding of thought processes comes mainly from the contemplation of our experiences and associated actions.

Nor does thinking lend itself easily to experimental study. It is true that numerous experimental approaches to the problem of thought have been made. But the results of such work have not infrequently proved rather inconclusive. It seems that experimenters have sometimes so interpreted experimental findings as to confirm their initial ideas about the *character* of thinking. It is, of course, easier to find confirming instances of one's theory than to submit it to a truly rigorous test. Thus, some *hypotheses* concerning the nature of thinking have found a measure of *confirmation*. But so also have rival hypotheses. For instance, in the controversy over *imageless thought*, those believed that it occurred found it to occur, but those who believed that there was no such thing could find no evidence of it. *Introspection* is not a dependable tool of genuine experimentation.

It has been said that thinking may be regarded as a '*bi-polar process*'. Reasoning, one important aspect of thinking, is at the one extreme. Imagination: practical, social, artistic, and scientific, is at the other extreme. No doubt, there is no clear dividing line between the two; nevertheless the distinction is a useful one.

Reasoning is *deductive thinking*, mathematically and *logically analysable* and precise. In principle, therefore, it can be imitated by mechanical and electrical *artefacts*. Imagination, inventive thinking, is *capricious* and unaccountable. Can *it* be imitated by machine too? We shall discuss this question presently.

A *thought process* is a more precise term than thinking. It restricts the field to those experiences of thinking which can be said to have some feature of completeness about them: a definite beginning and a definite end. A thought process has reasoning and imaginative aspects; but these fit into a more or less distinct whole.

The difference between the solving of a problem and a thought process is one of degree of *overtness*. It is a *moot* point, and partly a mere matter of the use of words, whether problem-solving in the narrow sense of the term always involves thinking of some kind. It may be argued that when a human being solves a problem, the inevitable implication is that he thinks. At any rate, problem-solving, in the everyday sense of the term, goes together with thought. A thought process may be regarded as a process of solving a problem in a manner which makes the attempts, the trials, the errors, and the successful solution hidden from direct observation. Thought processes are *vicarious* or *implicit* problem-solving processes."

The words and phrases that we still do not understand are: imagery; concept formation; character of thinking; hypotheses; confirmation, imageless thought; bipolar process; deductive thinking; logically analysable; artefacts; capricious overtness; moot point; vicarious; implicit.

In attempting to work out the meanings of these words, if the general context does not help, there are three main stages. First, try to think of any word you know which resembles the word that has held you up. This may be a familiar, everyday word or it may be a Latin or Greek root. In most cases this will give at least some general clue to the meaning. Second, bearing this in mind, study the word again in its context. Third, attempt to replace it by another word or phrase derived from your thinking at the first stage.

This process becomes clearer if we look at some actual examples.

Confirmation

Stage 1 : Everyone is familiar with the word "firm", meaning fixed, stable, steady. "Con" is a common prefix meaning together or with.

Stage 2: Context—"Thus, some hypotheses concerning the nature of thinking have found a measure of confirmation."

Stage 3: Thus, some hypotheses concerning the nature of thinking have to a certain extent been fixed, made firm, made reliable and therefore agreed upon.

Conclusion—confirmation most probably means agreement.

Bi-Polar Process

Stage 1 : We are familiar with the terms "north pole" and "south pole". Bi- is a common prefix meaning two.

Stage 2: "Thinking may be regarded as a '*bi-polar process*'. Reasoning . . . is at one extreme. Imagination . . . is at the other extreme."

Stage 3: The north and south poles are at the two extremes of the words. Thinking may be regarded as a process ranging between the extreme of reasoning and the extreme of imagination.

Conclusion—a bi-polar process is a process which has two extremes.

Hypotheses

Stage 1 : A knowledge of Greek helps here, but let us assume that we are ignorant of the language.

Stage 2: "It is, of course, easier to find confirming instances of one's theory than to submit it to a truly rigorous test. Thus, some hypotheses concerning the nature of thinking have found a measure of confirmation."

Stage 3: The first sentence mentions "confirming instances of one's theory". The second sentence says, "some hypotheses . . . have found a measure of confirmation". The two sentences are linked by the word "thus". There must, therefore, be a relationship between theories and hypotheses. From the context we can deduce that, because some hypotheses need confirmation, they are probably suppositions which form the *basis* of ideas.

Anyone who is uncertain of the meaning of any of the other underlined words in the above passage will benefit from a few minutes spent in working out their meanings in this way. The correct definitions should then be verified in a good dictionary. Dictionaries vary in reliability, and confusion can easily arise if the wrong dictionary is consulted. Generally speaking the Oxford dictionaries are the best for literary definitions and the history of words, but Chambers's Twentieth Century dictionary is probably better for scientific words. The more specialised the material the more the reader should use the particular subject dictionaries that are available, e.g. those published by Penguin Books on psychology, biology, art and music, etc.

When you have learned a new word, keep it in mind and note how it can be used in different contexts. Be ready to recognise it whenever it appears. If you *can* use a new word naturally in your thinking, writing or speaking, then do so, but let the new word come naturally. Do not make a strained effort to reform your thoughts or rephrase your sentences. In some cases, if you are unable to find a use for a new word it may prove to be one of those redundant words which far too many writers use to give "tone" to their writing. If you prefer to use "find out" instead of "ascertain"; "go" instead of "proceed"; "need" instead of "require", it does not mean that your vocabulary is weak but rather that you have good taste and a sensitivity about words.

Some people try to extend their vocabularies by deliberately studying lists of words or browsing through dictionaries. This method has its uses but, in general, it is better to devote the time to extending both the amount and the range of one's reading. In this way new words will be constantly learned and the reader will have the advantage of noting how they are used in different contexts, as well as becoming familiar with different patterns of presentation.

In trying to increase vocabulary by extending the range and amount of one's reading the main thing to remember is that considerable care must always be taken in choosing the right kind of book. This is of particular importance if the subject-matter is concerned with a completely unfamiliar discipline, and is largely a matter of common-sense. If the reader will bear in mind that learning is always most success-ful when one goes from the known to the unknown, from the familiar to the unfamiliar, he is unlikely to find himself floundering out of his depth.

The purpose of this chapter has not been to present a full course in vocabulary improvement but to stress the im-portance of vocabulary to anyone who wishes to improve his reading. Anyone who knows or even suspects that his vocabu-lary is weak should regard vocabulary work as a prime essential. "Work" is probably not the correct word here. "Interest" is probably better. Learning *about* words as well as learning words and thus bettering our powers of com-munication is an essential of life. Be word conscious; try to work out meanings for yourself; use the dictionary properly; read more, read widely, select carefully and develop a self-confidence in tackling "difficult books".

CHAPTER 10

Skimming and Scanning

OCCASIONALLY a magazine article mentions a reading demonstration where it is claimed that a properly trained reader can read at a rate of several thousand words a minute. Some gullible people with ever-increasing loads of written material on their hands and on their consciences jump to the conclusion that there is some magic technique or device which can miraculously transform the 200 word a minute slogger into a super-reader who digests whole pages at a glance, finishes the morning paper before his first cup of coffee and never returns home in the evening with a bulging brief-case of reading matter that he has failed to find time for during the day.

Whether or not this is possible depends entirely on the meaning we attach to the word "read". We have already defined the broad purpose of reading—we read to understand. But we have to remember that this is a very broad purpose. The speed at which we read obviously depends on whether we want to understand *all* the facts or only some of them.

Sometimes there is only *one* item of information that we want from a particular page and it can be found easily in a second or two. If reading is the process of getting the information we need from printed pages and understanding it, we can, in a sense, be said to have "read" the page when we have understood the single item of information we needed. Or imagine that we are trying to decide where to go for our holidays and wish to narrow down the choice. We consult four or more books on different countries. All that is needed is a *general* idea of the places concerned. For the moment we do not want to assimilate all the details about the reredos in the chapel of a remote mountain village in Italy. Consequently, one evening's reading would probably be sufficient for us to get the information we want from these books, and our reading speed would be something over a thousand words a minute with adequate comprehension.

With this kind of definition, reading at very high speeds of thousands of words a minute is possible in certain circumstances. But is it fair to call such an activity "reading"? To make the word "reading" meaningful we need to divide up the reading process into different techniques and call them by different names. The efficient reader is the person who is proficient in all these techniques—and extremely rapid reading is only one technique designed to be used for clearly defined purposes.

When we read four books in an evening it is better to refer to the activity as "skimming". The word is familiar and widely, though often wrongly, used. "I'll just skim through the paper," someone says. What does he mean? In many cases he means that he is going to take refuge behind a newspaper and glance somewhat vaguely down some of the pages in the hope of picking out something of interest. Sometimes he will succeed, sometimes not.

"Have you read this book?" "Well, I skimmed through it last night. It's very good." What does this mean? If it is a novel it probably means that the reader has picked up a fair idea of the plot. If it is a non-fiction book it means that the reader has thumbed through parts of it, lighted on one or two sections that he enjoyed, and then it was time for bed.

These activities are best described as "skimming through". But when an efficient reader uses the expression "skimming" he is referring to a well-defined reading skill which involves the judicious and selective skipping of non-essential or of less essential matter. In other words it means picking out the main facts and leaving the subsidiary details alone in order to get the essence of the material without reading all of it. There is nothing vague or casual about skimming. "The art of reading is to skip judiciously," wrote Philip Hamerton in the nineteenth century. The statement contains a great deal more truth if we amend it slightly so that it reads: "*One of the arts of reading is to skip judiciously.*"

At this stage many people might raise objections about the value of skimming. "It's no good for my kind of reading," they say. "In my job every word counts and sometimes every comma. I can't do my work properly by missing bits out judiciously or otherwise." It is true that there are certain forms of writing, legal documents, for instance, where the placing of a comma or the choice of a particular pronoun are matters for long and serious consideration. But can one talk about *my* kind of reading? Surely no one with an intelligent and enquiring mind can deliberately limit his choice of reading-matter to one single kind of reading. If cultivating the technique of skimming for other kinds of reading means that adequate time is available for close and intensive reading, then the effort has not been wasted.

Although there are certain kinds of reading where every word counts, it is still true that in most kinds of reading almost everyone skims to a slight degree whether he is aware of it or not. English is a language in which several words sometimes need to be used to express a single meaning. For example, if I say "I love" the single idea has to be expressed in two words. But in a language like Latin where articles and pronouns are joined on to other words I can say just "Amo". This does not mean that many articles, pronouns and prepositions are superfluous in English, but certainly for most reading, something like a quarter of the words in any one paragraph are of very minor importance, as was shown in the example "Cheeseparing on Books" in Chapter 4.

It is not suggested that we should begin a movement to reform the English language by declaring certain words obsolete. The point is that because it is possible to get the *full* meaning by paying only a fleeting attention to something between a quarter and a third of the words, most practised readers skim, probably unconsciously, over a quarter of the words in their reading matter.

Whether most people do it efficiently or not is a different matter. The purpose of this chapter is to suggest ways in which skimming may be practised so that it becomes an effective and reliable skill which can and ought to be used deliberately for specific purposes.

What are the purposes of skimming? Each person has to decide for himself the purposes for which he is reading, but to give an idea of the kinds of situations where skimming can be effectively used we can divide the technique up and call the two processes *Complete Skimming* and *Partial Skimming*.

Complete Skimming

is a very rapid way of getting information from print and there are many situations in which it can be used. Complete skimming means that literally *all* the details are disregarded. The reader is concerned *only* with the main theme and spends no time at all on examples, explanations, or the style of the book. In what circumstances would a reader wish to deal with reading matter in this way? In many cases the circumstances would arise when someone is looking through a book before reading it in more detail. He would do this because, if the reader has the author's main theme and point of view in mind before reading the material more fully, he can often read it with more advantage and understanding. Time spent on reconnaisance is seldom wasted. The statement is as true of reading as it is of military campaigns. Most pieces of writing are better understood when a preliminary survey of them has been made.

Another situation may arise when the book has already been read in detail and the student or reader wishes to refresh his mind about the author's treatment of the subject *as a whole*. If he has studied the book properly in the first place he should not need the examples and details, the main facts ought to be quite sufficient to recall the details that reinforce them.

In the rush of modern life the time factor is sometimes more important than anything else. If a business man finds himself due at a meeting in 15 minutes and has not found the time to read the 10,000 word report which is going to be discussed there, he has no option but to use the complete skimming technique. In such a situation worries about whether he is missing some interesting example or detail have no place.

Complete skimming is also frequently used when a subject is being studied which necessitates getting information from a large number of books. In reading history, for example, it often happens that the student starts to read a book and after a chapter or so realises that the author is being particularly long winded and that much of what he has to say is irrelevant to the needs of the reader. If in these circumstances the reader still wishes to know the writer's general point of view, then he is advised to skim the book rather than persevere with detailed reading which might prove a waste of time. Such a situation need not occur if the reader would make a habit of skimming at least part of each book before deciding whether to read it thoroughly.

Partial Skimming

can be defined as complete skimming with reservations. In partial skimming, as in complete skimming, the book is read so that the main theme becomes clear, but whenever any of the *details* are of value to the reader he slows down his rapid skimming rate and reads more intensively. A technique such as this would be used when the reader is well acquainted with both subject and author. He does not wish to waste time reading material with which he is already familiar, but when some new point is made he will want to know about it in detail. The technique is really a combination of complete skimming and any other reading techniques which are appropriate to the reader's needs at particular places in the book. The reading of the travel books mentioned earlier in this chapter is an example of when partial skimming would be appropriate. The reader's main need would be for background information, but, occasionally, particular details would also be relevant.

The objections most frequently levelled against skimming techniques are, first, that reading at a very high speed must increase the chances of missing something of vital importance, and, second, that if a book is skimmed the whole of the atmosphere and style are lost. The answer to the first objection is that if the skimming is done properly the chances of missing something of *vital importance* are no greater than if the entire book is read slowly. Speed and inaccuracy do not necessarily go together and slowness and carefulness cannot be said to go together either. The whole thing depends on whether the skimming is done efficiently or not.

The answer to the second question is that in the kinds of circumstances outlined above the reader does not want the style or atmosphere of the book. He is concerned only with its gist. If a reader wishes to appreciate the author's style or listen to the delicate rhythms of his sentences or savour the words he uses or study the details or examples, then he would not be skimming the book anyway—except as a preliminary—in which case he would be able to do these things when he reads the book more intensively.

Reading material should be skimmed whenever time, presentation, needs and purposes justify such a reading method. No one can lay down definite rules about when skimming techniques should be used because their use depends on too many variables. An efficient reader studying one book might, in the course of his reading, use complete and partial skimming techniques, intensive reading techniques and half a dozen other techniques. When he uses them depends on his personal needs, the kind of material he is reading and the kind of person he is.

The technique of efficient skimming depends primarily on the reader's ability to distinguish accurately and rapidly between what is of real importance to him and what is of less importance. In particular it depends on the reader's complete familiarity with the ways in which writers present different kinds of information.

A thorough understanding of the structure of paragraphs is the key to effective skimming. As mentioned before, most paragraphs contain a topic sentence or a principal idea which can, if necessary, be quickly summarised into a topic sentence by the reader. A topic sentence tends to occur much more frequently at the beginning or the end of a paragraph than in the middle. This is generally true of most written material, and if we examine a number of paragraphs in different kinds of books we find that the introductory and concluding parts tend to deal chiefly with essentials, broadly treated, and the middle section contains the details.

If the reader can immediately isolate the topic sentence in each paragraph and read *only* the topic sentences it follows that he will finish the book or article rapidly and have a very sound idea of the main theme of the material. Such a method of reading might be sufficient for his purposes and he can then put the book aside. Or, having skimmed the book, he might wish to read it all or certain sections of it in greater detail. In this case his preliminary skimming will be of great value in helping him to understand the details in their correct context.

Skimming then depends largely on learning to isolate rapidly and accurately the topic sentences of paragraphs. Generally speaking, a topic sentence does not often occur in the middle of a paragraph, and the tendency is for it to come at the beginning of a paragraph rather than at the end. Consequently, if we were really in a hurry and decided to read only the first sentence of each paragraph in a book we should find in most cases sufficient information to enable us to connect the principal ideas mentioned in the writing so that the main theme could be followed.

If the first sentence of each paragraph was in fact the topic sentence almost any book susceptible to skimming could be skimmed effectively by reading only the first sentences of the paragraphs. However, because topic sentences do not always occur in such a prominent position, a much more reliable method is needed. The likelihood of the first sentence being a topic sentence is strong enough for us to begin skimming by reading only the first sentences of paragraphs, but in the event of any breakdowns in the continuity of thought when the topic sentence is not at the beginning we must be capable of isolating the main idea of the paragraph rapidly and accurately.

The reader who is concentrating on the onward progression of thought will detect these breakdowns in continuity immediately. When such a breakdown occurs and the reader knows that the first sentence of a particular paragraph is not a topic sentence, he will (in many cases) find that the first, or one of the first words in the sentence, is a pronoun. If it is a pronoun the end of the *preceding* paragraph will frequently fill the gap in the continuity.

Sometimes the breakdown is not so easy to put right. If the reader tries the above method and fails, he is advised to return to the obscure sentence, formulate a question from it and then deliberately search for the answer. When that has been found he can continue the process of skimming by continuing to read only the first sentence of each paragraph until another breakdown in the continuity of thought occurs.

This method is not by any means foolproof. But it is an exceptionally good starting point for the reader who wishes to practise the technique of skimming. Many readers who have never tried this method of picking out main ideas and completely ignoring details are surprised to find how much information can be rapidly gained by it. They are also surprised to find, after practice, how the writer's main ideas seem to jump from the page whether or not they are contained in the first sentences of the paragraphs.

Apart from the technique of concentrating only on topic sentences the reader must also learn to use everything contained in the material he is skimming that can help him to attain his end of picking out and understanding the main ideas. If he is reading a book, the list of contents, the introduction, the summary at the end, the chapter titles and subtitles can all help if they are used properly. Even if the material is only a fairly short article much can be gained by trying to see it *as a whole* before the actual reading begins. Study the title and the sub-headings. Try to find the focal point of emphasis. Ask questions. Look for the answers and find them. Above all get involved in the subject.

When starting the actual reading begin with a definite plan such as the first sentence method outlined above. But regard it as a flexible method. As you get involved in the reading and begin to see how the author presents his thoughts and arranges the facts within the paragraphs you will find that it is immediately obvious whether or not the first sentence of a paragraph is a topic sentence, and if it is not it will be a matter of only a second or two to find the required sentence.

Skimming is a time-saving technique and to get the most benefit from it it is a good plan, particularly when practising, to read according to a definite schedule. This helps to give the determination that is necessary for picking out the main facts accurately and rapidly.

Here is an example of how this skimming technique might

be used with an actual book—*The Social Psychology of Industry* by J. A. C. Brown. Let us divide up the whole process into stages and consider the various points that arise.

First we wish to know whether or not it is worth our while reading the book. We need therefore to get some basic information rapidly. The front cover merely gives us the title of the book and the name of the author. Before we decide to spend time on it we need further information about both. We turn then to the title page inside the book where the main title is usually given a subsidiary heading. In this case it is "Human Relations in the Factory". Next, the author. Who is he? What are his qualifications? Why is he writing this book? Information about the author is some-times given at the beginning of the book, more often it is found on the back cover as it is here. We learn :

"James A. C. Brown was born in Edinburgh in 1911. After taking a degree in medicine at Edinburgh University, he travelled and studied in many European countries and during the war was a Specialist in Psychiatry in the Middle East. In addition to practising psychiatry in the army, he has also had experience in mental hospitals, prisons, and on selection boards. Becoming predominantly interested in the normal individual's adjustment to society, he joined a large industrial concern after the war, in which he worked for seven years. Although brought up in a school of thought which regarded mental illness mainly as an individual and biological prob-lem, he now regards it as basically a social one and takes the view that the mental conflicts of the neurotic are in large measure induced by the sick society in which he lives. For this reason he feels that the efficiency of industry cannot be measured solely in terms of the amount of goods it produces or its financial profits; we must also consider at what cost of health and happiness the goods were produced. The present book is an attempt to express this point of view.

Dr Brown has written several other books on psychiatry and psychology, amongst them *The Distressed Mind* and *The Evolution of Society*."

At this stage if we are interested in industry we should probably decide to read the book and that the author is admirably qualified to write on the subject.

As well as giving us Dr. Brown's qualifications, the long paragraph we have just read sets out his purpose in writing the book. This purpose is all-important. Now that we know it we can get the right mental set for reading the book. We are, even at this stage, looking for an answer to the question : "At what cost of health and happiness are our industrial goods produced?" We also know that we shall find the answer by studying human relations in the factory.

Can we before starting on the text reinforce the information we have already got? Most books contain a brief account of the contents. Sometimes this is a publisher's blurb, a mere advertising eulogy extolling the author's merits. Sometimes, as in this case, it is a more objective statement of the book's aims.

"In recent years it is becoming increasingly apparent that the classical approach to industrial psychology is inadequate. This approach regarded the worker primarily as a machine to be studied by the techniques of physiological psychology and as an isolated individual whose aptitudes caused him to be suited or unsuited for a given job. The results obtained by such an approach are not necessarily wrong, but, as Elton Mayo demonstrated conclusively more than twenty years ago, they are bound to be incomplete because the 'isolated' human being is a fiction. Since each individual is a member of society and each worker a member of a working group, the attitudes of these groups are bound to play a large part in influencing his behaviour both as citizen and worker.

This book makes no attempt to replace other text-books on industrial psychology; it should rather be regarded as an attempt to supply the reader with an understanding of the social background of industry. Believing that if we begin with the wrong assumptions no amount of accurate research can produce the correct answers, the author has tried to discuss such fundamental questions as : what is human nature? what causes men to work? what is morale? And what influence has the nature of industrial work upon the mental health of the individual worker and his community?"

From these two paragraphs we can quickly get some valuable information about the book and the author's viewpoint. First we learn that the classical approach to industrial psychology (i.e. regarding the worker primarily as a machine) is inadequate. Second, we learn that the aim of the book is to supply the reader with an understanding of the social background of industry and to discuss such questions as:

What is human nature?
What causes men to work?
What is morale?
What influence has the nature of industrial work upon the mental health of the individual worker and his community?

Already specific questions are demanding answers. Some we shall formulate for ourselves, e.g. Why is the classical approach to industrial psychology inadequate? Others, such as those above, are mentioned specifically.

As well as information about the author and the book in general, most books have a foreword or an introduction or both. In this case we have both. Here is the editorial foreword. Read it quickly, bearing in mind that your object in so doing is to pick out any important facts which will help you to read the book with adequate understanding.

Editorial Foreword

"Industrial psychology, in its early days, nearly captured from economics the right to the title of the most dismal of the sciences. It vied with economics in giving the impression that by diligent and conscientious work the scientist could reduce the romantic story of man's technological achievements to a compact mass of dry-as-dust statistics. The figures produced by the industrial psychologists proved beyond all doubt that accidents and fatigue could be reduced, that output and earnings could be augmented, by the simplest of devices. Much of this could be done merely by changes in lighting, heating, and ventilation. Still more could be effected by changes in factory layout, by the redesign of machines, by time-and-motion study, and by more ingenious 'incentives'. Men could be scientifically trained to produce more and more by doing less and less; and they could do all this the more cheerfully to an accompaniment of music while they worked. But when the figures were all added up they somehow left the impression that the ultimate goal of these endeavours was the creation of an ideal factory fashioned in the style (to use the words of the author of this book) of a 'model cow-house'—the milch cows of which were, of course, the industrial workers.

The patient and placid cows were not impressed. To them it seemed all too true to be good. It seemed, too, to miss something out. The industrial psychologists and the scientific managers had to think again. They *did* think again and they thought to good effect. What was missing, they discovered first of all, was an adequate conception of the individual worker as an ordinary human being. Hitherto they had thought of workers in the mass as a vast number of little 'economic men'—each impelled by an irresistible inner force to seek the maximum wage at a minimum effort. True, it had long been known that men in battle or in love are moved to great endeavours by other and more eccentric motives; but this had been supposed to be one of the curiosities of life outside the province proper to the scientist. Still, being honest scientists, they took another look at human nature and at actual human motives. They discovered the individual human being. In the course of doing this they made a second discovery. They hit on 'the working group'. This, too, it might be said, was but another spectacular rediscovery of the obvious; but, after the event, so many revolutionary findings take on this appearance. That 'man is a social animal' had been taken so much for granted in general that no one had stopped to think what this might mean in particular situations. A new chapter in the history of industrial psychology was opened when the scientist began to inquire what was implied by the sociability of man in the workshop situation.

The fact of 'informal organisation' and of its impact upon the motivation of the individual then came as a blinding revelation. Industrial Psychology ceased to be a minor branch of applied physiology or of 'industrial engineering' and became a major branch of social psychology.

The redirection of scientific interest towards social issues happily coincided with a trend in industry towards greater mutual understanding than had hitherto been displayed between the two 'sides'. Enlightened management can no longer be accused of treating the worker as the milch cow of the system; and organised labour can no longer be said to lack interest in the problems of management. On both sides, too, there is a greater disposition to look at the needs of an industry with some regard to the needs of the community as a whole, and to think of that industry, whether nationalised or not, as a public service. Practical good sense, serviced by this new industrial psychology, may yet accomplish in a quiet way an industrial revolution as momentous as any industrial revolution in the past.

This new chapter in industrial psychology is still being written. It is a chapter full of promise. The story of the emergence of a brighter prospect is told in this book. It is told by one who enjoys a unique combination of qualifications to write it : impressive erudition, relevant practical experience in industry, and that humane understanding which alone can breathe freshness and life into the desiccated figures of research reports."

A very rapid reading of this foreword should provide three important facts. First, the passage goes into more detail about why the classical approach to industrial psychology is inadequate. Second, it points out that the *new* industrial psychology is largely concerned with "the sociability of man in the workshop situation" and is therefore a major branch of social psychology rather than as in the past a minor branch of applied physiology or of "industrial engineering". Third, we learn that this redirection of industrial psychology coincides with a trend towards a greater mutual understanding between management and workers.

Here is the author's Introduction :

Introduction

"The title of this book adequately indicates its scope. It is concerned basically with the emotional aspects of human inter-relationships in industry, and lays no claim to be a study of industrial psychology as such. Nor does it set out specifically to give practical details of what might be done to improve conditions in industry. What I have tried to do is to put forward for the consideration of the factory manager, the personnel manager, the time and motion engineer, and the interested layman certain fundamental aspects of 'human nature' and social organisation which must be taken into account by anyone attempting to reorganise factory life.

In a book which touches on such varied subjects as psychology, history, medicine, anthropology, economics, and the practice of management, much of what is said will appear painfully elementary to those with expert knowledge of one or other of these subjects. I can only hope that it does not also appear erroneous."

Here again in a very short time we can learn : first, that the book is not a study of industrial psychology. It is concerned basically with the emotional aspects of human inter-relationships in industry and deals with certain fundamental aspects of "human nature" and social organisation which must be taken into account by anyone attempting to re-organise factory life. Second, that the book touches on a variety of subjects such as : psychology, history, medicine, anthropology, economics and the practice of management. Because of this wide variety of subjects they are treated in a fairly elementary manner.

We have already gained a considerable amount of information about the book before starting on the text. One further thing needs to be done in this preliminary survey and that is to try to find out how the author has organised his material. The easiest starting point is to look closely at the table of contents. Here it is :

From this table of contents the reader will see that some of the questions that have already formed in his mind are dealt with in specific chapters, e.g. What is human nature? What causes men to work? At this stage someone who is already well informed about the kinds of topics that are dealt with in this book might turn to one of the chapters in which he is particularly interested or look up a point in the index to note how the author deals with it.

This analysis of introductions and forewords has been done in some detail, but in fact it should take only a few minutes to collect, in this way, a considerable amount of material before looking at the text itself. From this information the reader ought to be able to determine his needs and purposes in reading the book. He might at this stage decide that he needs only to skim the book. Does he then begin at Chapter 1 and go through the book concentrating on the topic sentences? To begin at the beginning is not necessarily the best starting point particularly if the reader wants to pick out the main points as quickly as possible. The index shows us that Chapter 10 contains a summary and conclusions and in some cases the reader who has decided to skim the book might do it much more efficiently if he starts there.

Many people will object to this suggestion. "The purpose of a summary", they say, "is to remind the reader of the main points that have been mentioned so that everything falls into perspective at the end, and to assist his memory of these points. Also, the purpose of a conclusion is to some extent lost if the reader does not follow the argument through and does not consider the evidence. A conclusion stated baldly without accompanying evidence and argument is unlikely to be assessed properly by the reader and consequently there is at least a possibility of prejudice coming in."

These are perfectly reasonable points, but they have to be seen in perspective. Our purpose in reading is to understand, and any methods we use to make that understanding quicker and more accurate are good methods. So it is at least worth investigating how much help can be obtained by looking, in some cases, at the summary and conclusions *before* reading the book in detail or skimming it. It is reasonable to say that if reading the summary and conclusions *first* helps the reader to get involved in the book, to follow the author's line of thought more clearly, to formulate specific questions and find the answers in the text without filling his head with prejudice, then it is perfectly justifiable.

However, even if the book is being skimmed, it is not usually sufficient to read only summaries and conclusions. The reader must still make himself familiar with the way the author treats his subject. The rapid reading of the text with attention fixed on main ideas and topic sentences is a necessary part of the technique of skimming. To do this properly the reader must practice, and for this purpose newspapers are admirable. The *Reader's Digest* type of publication should not, however, be used for skimming practice because in many cases the articles and "potted" books represent the results of an editorial skimming process. The reader is in fact being presented with the main ideas, and the less essential matter has already been cut out.

One interesting point that is noticeable about complete skimming is that, when more detailed reading follows skimming, it is quite often found that there is little of any real value to add to the results of the skimming. Authors who never waffle are few and far between. An acute observer once expressed it neatly by saying, "Much of the wisdom of the world is contained in books and so is much of the nonsense."

Finally, it must be emphasised that, although Dr Brown's book has been selected for a small amount of analysis in a chapter entitled "Skimming", it is not being suggested that *The Social Psychology of Industry* is a book which should be skimmed rather than read in detail. It is a valuable book with which people concerned with industry ought to be familiar.

Scanning

"Knowledge is of two kinds", said Dr. Johnson. "We know a subject ourselves or we know where we can find information upon it." He could well have added, "And *how* to find information upon it." Finding specific information involves scanning. This means looking very rapidly through printed matter to find the answer to a particular question or to locate a particular passage. The technique is often confused with skimming and sometimes the two terms are used interchangeably. But, correctly used, scanning refers to a deliberate search for some specific item, as when we say, "I scanned the horizon". The implication here is that we were looking for some particular person or thing.

Scanning, then, is used only when we wish to find some specific information. The act of reading does not occur until the place where the information is located has been found. When we look up a number in a telephone book, or a word in a dictionary, we scan the book.

Most adults ought to be able to find specific information in a directory or a dictionary with maximum speed and efficiency. They should be able to locate the place in a very few seconds and then assimilate the information with sufficient accuracy to fulfil their purpose. But *can* most people do this even at such an elementary level? It is surprising, for instance, how many people look up a telephone number and then dial it incorrectly. It is also surprising how many people look up a word in a dictionary, select one of its meanings at random, return to the text, find that it is the wrong meaning and then go through the whole process again at a similar level of inefficiency.

A different form of scanning is when the reader is faced with a whole book or a full-length report and wishes to extract from the material information about one single topic, or about a limited number of topics. In many cases he will be able to use the index, look up the references given by scanning the appropriate page, and then read more intently the information relevant to his purposes. For instance, if after reading Dr. Brown's book we wish to refresh our memory of what is said about the criticism of Elton Mayo's work, it is a simple matter to look up Mayo in the index and locate the particular page. If there were no index we should turn to the table of contents, locate the chapter dealing with Elton Mayo and then scan it until we found the relevant passages.

Note that the word used here is scan, not skim. How exactly do we scan? Consider what happens when you look up a number in a directory or a word in a dictionary. You find it quickly for three reasons. First, you know where to look for it. Second, you know exactly what you are looking for. Third, you are for the moment uninterested in anything else. What you do when you find the information is, of course, another matter. The scanning technique has then finished and a different reading technique appropriate to the circumstances must be used. The whole value of scanning is lost if, when the information is found, it cannot for some reason be properly assimilated. Scanning is a means to an end, most certainly not an end in itself.

Can the three reasons why a number can be found rapidly in a telephone book be given a much more general application? If we consider what is implied by these three reasons we see that the second and third mean that the reader has got the right mental set and a high degree of motivation. He is intent on finding the information he requires and consequently he knows roughly the kinds of words that are likely to be used when that information is given. For instance, if we are scanning a particular section of Dr. Brown's book looking for passages relating to the criticism of Elton Mayo's researches, the words that we would keep firmly in mind would be "Elton Mayo" and "criticism". Other related words would be "validity", "research", "objection", etc. With these words firmly in mind finding the relevant passages is a matter of certainty, not of luck. The more definite our mental set the more quickly we shall succeed in finding the information because we shall not be *reading* the lines through which we are searching. Our eyes will run over several lines at a time and we shall not stop to read until pulled up sharply by one or other of the words that we have in mind.

Scanning Exercise

The answers to the following questions can be found in Chapters 1–10 in this book. Adapting the techniques given in this chapter, find first the page and paragraph where the information can be found and then the answer to the question. Before starting to scan the book think for a few moments exactly how you are going to get this information in the shortest possible time. Remember that time spent on reconnaissance is seldom wasted, and that a flexible but deliberate method of setting about finding information is much more rapid and efficient than merely looking hopefully through the material.

Questions

1. What was the date of the Act for creating and establishing a Post Office?
2. Who said, "The stuff with which we work is the fabric of men's minds"?
3. Is this quotation correct : "Knowledge is of two kinds; we know a subject ourselves or we know where we can find information about it"?
4. What are surface isobars?
5. Who wrote *Sense and Nonsense in Psychology*?
6. *The Social Psychology of Industry* was written by Dr. James A. C. Brown. What other books has he written?
7. How many daily newspapers are there in Los Angeles?
8. What percentage of reading time is spent in actual eye movement?

9. When was the first Annual World Meteorological Day?
10. Who wrote these lines:

> "Bookful blockhead, ignorantly read,
> With loads of learned lumber in his head."

11. Who started the London Penny Post?
12. How much does it cost to give a child an intelligence test and score it?
13. What is a tachistoscope?
14. Who wrote *The Uses of Literacy*?

CHAPTER 11

Remembering

CAN you, without refreshing your memory, give the gist of one single article or news item in this morning's newspaper? If you cannot, how long did you spend *looking* at the newspaper? And do you consider that it was time well spent? How much can you remember about the last book you read? Can you give the gist of that? Can you confidently recall one notable chapter and state briefly and accurately its main theme?

If these questions cause the reader even a twinge of embarrassment, then it is fairly certain that he is not using his memory to the best advantage. And that means that he is not tackling his reading in an efficient manner.

If a reader is unable to retain the facts and ideas he gets from print, then much of his time is being wasted. The purpose of this chapter is to discuss some particular points about remembering and to suggest how the reader can increase the efficiency of his memory by making himself aware of the ways in which he can use his memory most effectively. It is not a question of improving the memory intrinsically, but rather of learning how to organise and manage the particular memory one has.

The term "a good memory" is frequently used to refer to the kind of memory which retains and recalls the actual words, or a near approximation of them, which have been used in certain connections. Verbal memory, as this is called, is not nearly as useful as it might appear because although the actual words may be remembered it does not therefore follow that they have also been understood.

Remembering is far from being just a process of mechanical reproduction. The memory records far more than can be recalled. Even overhearing an unintelligible language leaves some traces on the mind or nervous system, and it is indeed possible that we remember everything. This is important because although the ability to recall with accuracy is obviously a useful talent, there are "subconscious" factors which must also be taken into account when we consider the results of reading. Even if we forget all the details about a book—its style, purpose, author, when we read it, etc.—the material may still have affected our general outlook. However bad or good a person's verbal memory may be, all that he has read is likely in some measure to affect his life.

It must therefore be emphasised that the first essential in remembering is the ability to get the facts straight. This ability was commented on at some length in previous chapters when we considered the fundamental importance of reading for meaning and assimilating main ideas accurately. It was pointed out then that reading is a process of discrimination. Memory is also selective. When it works well it sorts out whatever is relevant for a particular purpose, and also reshapes the material so as to make it suitable for the purpose for which it is recalled.

We could put this in a different way by saying that forgetting is as necessary as remembering. If we did not forget we could not really remember, and many facts are just not worth remembering. No one consciously remembers everything. For most of us it is difficult to remember what we had for lunch a week ago, and hardly anyone can reel off the menus for the last month. The fact that we cannot do this does not necessarily mean that we have bad memories. It means only that we have no real purpose in remembering all the details of last month's meals, and, consequently, we forget them.

If we are to consider the problems of remembering, we must therefore start by considering the problems of selection. Some people do not, at first, accept this as a satisfactory basis. They say, "In my kind of reading I can't afford to select. Every little thing counts. It's all or nothing as far as I'm concerned." This sort of objection does not stand up to much examination. All reading material is the result of selection and when, in turn, the reader selects from the material information appropriate to his needs and purposes, he is only continuing a process of selection that began a long time before.

A daily newspaper, for instance, is the result of a complicated process of selection. Reporters decide on details they consider important; news agencies select from this; news editors and sub-editors continue the work; the reader selects what he wants to read; and finally his mind does a further job of selection, compression, arrangement and integration.

Whether we have a good memory or not depends less on our ability to reproduce facts mechanically than on the ability of our mental faculties to organise the process of selection properly. This is really what is implied by the now familiar phrases "getting the main ideas", "reading for meaning", etc. The whole skill of remembering what we read depends on this process of proper selection, of retaining what is relevant and discarding what is irrelevant. A person might have an extremely good verbal memory, but if he is unable to select what is relevant for particular circumstances a valuable natural gift is going to waste.

A good verbal memory is an asset only when it is allied with other abilities and skills. The "verbal memory" recalls facts, but it is the "rational memory" which recalls different facts in a particular relationship with each other. Remembering must involve thinking if it is to be anything more than the mere mechanical reproduction of information. Consequently, the most important of these other abilities and skills is the ability to think. To think about information means to make that information meaningful, and usually it is made meaningful when it is linked to other information.

Selection alone is not enough, we need also to establish connections between the various items of information that we assimilate when we read. Generally speaking, the writer will already have done quite a lot of the work for us. He will, if he has done his job properly, have made his material meaningful *in general*. The reader's job is to make the material *personally* meaningful, that is, he must integrate new facts and ideas with the knowledge and experience that he already has. He must select the information he wishes to remember and then, or at the same time, he must think about it.

Let us look at this in a little more detail. We know that a writer presents his facts according to a definite pattern basically concerned with grouping similar facts or ideas together in clusters which tend to consist of one main point supported by a number of subsidiary points. The ideas are connected together in a logical sequence. This presentation is so that the information will be *generally* meaningful for as many people as possible. Obviously, if the writer was explaining his material separately to individual people, say in the form of letters, he would in each case alter his presentation according to the individual needs so that it would become *personally* meaningful to each one. Because the reader cannot expect books to be written for him personally, it is up to him to do this job of making the material personally meaningful. This job can be conveniently summarised into four divisions :

First, he must get to know the general pattern by involving himself in the reading and thinking with the author.

Second, he must pick out the author's main theme and the *principal* ideas that develop this theme.

Third, he must be able to summarise accurately and clearly in his own words the main points that the writer is making.

Fourth, he must be able to relate these main ideas to his own previous knowledge.

If the reader can become proficient in these skills—and they are all skills that can be practised and learned—he will find that remembering what he reads may have its difficulties, but that these difficulties can usually be overcome when the task is organised in an efficient way. He will also find that, if he continually emphasises to himself the importance of reading for meaning, many difficulties of remembering will resolve themselves automatically.

Remembering the main ideas is often only part of the job, and sooner or later we come up against the problem of having to remember a considerable number of details. The first thing that must be stressed here is that, in most cases, the hardest facts to remember are the isolated facts. Therefore, if a new fact can be connected with a group of previously known facts, the sooner the new fact will become meaningful and the better we shall retain it and be able to recall it.

Whenever a situation arises where isolated facts need to

be remembered we must always think in terms of *connection*. On the title-page of *Howard's End* E. M. Forster wrote the words, "Only Connect". They are as good advice as many a long chapter on understanding and memory. Only connect and more of the difficulties of remembering will disappear.

How does one connect? Remembering what we read begins with our psychological outlook, and the *will* to remember is probably the most important factor. We read to understand, but unless we positively want to understand we are not going to get very far. The will to remember depends largely on interest in the subject-matter. The more interested we are the more active our desire to remember and, consequently, the more likely we are to connect in a meaningful way any new knowledge with our previous knowledge.

Very little is known about what actually goes on in the brain when it receives information from print. Part of the process is "conscious" and part "subconscious" in the sense that a thought process started consciously can continue when the conscious attention is directed elsewhere. Experience shows us that "subconscious" organisation of information is often more efficient than its conscious equivalent. In some cases a difficult problem posed at bed-time can be solved "subconsciously" by the morning.

But whether we are talking about a conscious or a "subconscious" process of organisation of information the relevant point here is that whenever our interest is aroused by something we have read we almost invariably think about it on other occasions. This is because interest is largely a matter of intelligence and when we think about something we are really sorting the new information we have gained into the general pattern of our knowledge and experience. The less interested we are in what we read the less chance our minds have to organise the information systematically so that relevant items can be made available when we wish to recall them.

Generalisations about interest in different kinds of reading can be misleading because interests are personal and individual. What interests one person does not interest another, and consequently we can never say that some things are easier to remember than others.

Sooner or later reading matter which we originally thought to be interesting becomes boring. When this happens we must use our common sense. If information is not being assimilated it cannot, obviously, be remembered and time is being wasted. Boredom and fatigue usually become complicating factors when a reading schedule has unlimited duration. It is possible to concentrate on almost anything for a limited period of time, and so boredom and fatigue can often be dealt with by keeping the periods of work short. There is no reason why these periods should not be numerous provided that there are recreative periods between them. Of course, the definition of a "short" period depends on the subject-matter. Ten-minute periods might be quite long enough for committing to memory small items of information, but they would be too short for assimilating extended scientific explanations or philosophical arguments.

This brings us to the subject of "learning by heart", an ability which is not nearly so necessary as some people think. Generally speaking, it is probably better to know one's way about a considerable number of works on a particular subject so that the appropriate information can be found quickly when it is needed, than to spend time on committing a great deal to memory in the hope that it will be on tap at the right moment. The mind cannot compete with a reference library in accuracy, efficiency or comprehensiveness.

Many readers work on the principle that if they go on reading something over and over again they will eventually learn it. At first they are able to recall a few phrases, then the whole outline becomes familiar and they begin to concentrate on the gaps. Eventually after many hours of boredom the entire passage can be repeated word for word.

But repetition is by no means necessary for accurate remembering. A striking fact or a fact presented in a striking way and never repeated may never be forgotten. If a fact has to be remembered it is better to present it in a striking way to oneself by linking it with other knowledge in a meaningful way so as to give it its due measure of importance, than to go on repeating it so that, although the form of words may be remembered, the meaning and relevance are lost.

When understanding of the material is sufficient to supply a rational explanation to the reader he ought not to rely on learning by heart or memory tricks such as mnemonics.

A great deal of time is completely wasted in "learning by heart". Examiners, for instance, often set little more than a memory test, and much that has to be committed to memory is forgotten soon afterwards. The amount of information with which our minds become loaded during the examination years does not by its sheer quantity do any harm, but the waste of time and the boredom to which such "learning" can give rise are in no measure compensated by the relatively small benefit gained.

Attempts at memorising whole strings of information are often frustrating and boring. The rewards are usually small and complete accuracy is rare. It is much better to concentrate on getting the gist of the material accurately, making it meaningful to one's own knowledge and experience, and thinking about or practising its application. To spend time on working out what an example proves or illustrates is better than trying to remember the details of the example itself. When information becomes meaningful it is surprising how easily the actual details can be recalled. The reader who is in the habit of pausing in his reading, closing his eyes and attempting to repeat items word for word is usually wasting both time and energy. When strings of facts look as though they ought to be learned by heart the first stage should consist of working out some frame of reference which will give the facts a *meaning*.

This matter of assisting the memory by reading for the *whole* meaning can be illustrated by the different ways in which children are sometimes taught to learn poems by heart. When children learn a poem they are sometimes advised or even told to do it stanza by stanza, presumably because then the work can be broken up and some idea of progress gained. But, if the material cannot be broken up into *meaningful* sections, this method can be very uneconomical. If the *meaning* of the whole passage can be put over with sufficient impact then the details will very soon be learned, but if that initial impact is missing learning the details is going to be tedious.

It has been said earlier that the efficient reader is the one who constantly questions both before and during reading. Join this fact on to the others that have been mentioned here and we can see that to form questions, find meaningful answers, relate them to one's own knowledge, assess the importance of the information and its relevance and be able to summarise or re-phrase in one's own words the main points given is the basis for remembering what is read.

To summarise the whole of this chapter on remembering, it could be said that if a person learns to read efficiently he will find little difficulty in remembering *what he needs or wants to remember*. The basis of remembering is gaining an accurate and meaningful impression. The reader who has confidence in his ability to get the main ideas accurately from a piece of writing and to make them meaningful is likely to remember them. The more he thinks about them, the better he will remember and the more easily will he be able to recall them.

Practice can improve the ability to remember although it cannot alter the kind of memory a person has. Improving the memory means learning to make the best use of the memory one has. The following suggestions for practice can be carried out with almost any kind of written material :

1. Practise selecting what you *want* to remember. Quite a lot of facts are just not worth remembering. You *want* to have a memory like a sieve. You *want* a memory that will retain what you need and discard what you do not need. A sieve is an article of great value if it is used properly.
2. Practise picking out the main ideas in whatever you are reading. If what you read is to be remembered it must be meaningful, and the best way of making it so is to concentrate on the accurate assimilation of the writer's main ideas.
3. Practise thinking constructively when you read. A good approach to this is to bear in mind that knowledge depends to a large extent on asking the right questions. The reading process must to some extent be a process of formulating questions and assimilating the correct answers.

4. Test your ability to remember and develop confidence in it. If you read the newspaper yesterday morning and cannot remember a single headline in it or give the gist of a leader-page article, read today's paper with more determination. When you have finished the leader-page article try to recall the main points. Think about them and, if possible, talk about them. Tomorrow see if you can still give the gist of the article. If you fail look at the article again and try to find out why you have failed.

CHAPTER 12

Study Reading

WHEN we think of study reading we usually think in terms of text-books and the systematic learning of a particular discipline. There is, however, no need to limit study reading to the activities of a student undergoing a formal course of study. We are all students so long as our minds remain active. This is particularly true today when new realms of knowledge are constantly opening up, when specialisation demands knowledge and understanding of other disciplines and when it is necessary for almost all professional men to do at least some regular study reading to keep up with developments in their particular fields.

Study-reading, then, has considerably wider applications than the mere formal slogging through a text-book. It may relate to the study of books, or it may be concerned with articles in technical journals or the reading of papers presented to learned societies. In cases such as these efficient and economical reading is of the utmost necessity because few employers allow adequate time even for the necessary study reading which most responsible work entails.

Our first task must be to discover what study reading involves. In the first place there must be considerable emphasis on understanding and being able to recall all the main details and many of the subsidiary details as well. In such a context a word like "rapid" would only be used by a magician. In comparison with most other kinds of reading, study reading is necessarily very slow because it is concerned with details as well as main ideas.

In study reading two different processes can be isolated. One is a deductive process where we begin with a general statement and proceed to particular examples of its application. The other is an inductive process where we start by considering a number of facts and then proceed, by considering the relationship between these facts, to formulate, or to study the formulation of, a relevant conclusion. In skimming a book whose subject matter we are reasonably familiar with, it might in certain situations be necessary only to take a firm hold of the conclusion drawn from the facts in the case of induction or the generalised statement in the case of deduction. But in study reading, though our reading may begin with skimming it ought to end with a recall of all the details relevant to the reader's needs. Consequently, more than one reading technique must be used and for maximum efficiency it is necessary to have some sort of systematic approach.

The mention of a "systematic approach" affects different people in different ways. Some derive a feeling of security from the idea of being given an efficient study system, others become irritated at the thought that their own efficiency, built up possibly after years of trial and error, may be reduced if they allow themselves to be dragooned into using methods which, though admirable for some people, may not be applicable to everyone.

There is no rigid method of study reading which everyone can use effectively in the same way. It is up to each individual to formulate the method that is most effective for him. But, having decided which method is best, the reader ought, with necessary modifications according to circumstances, to be consistent about its use in all normal conditions of study reading. A constant switching about from one system to another cannot be efficient.

This chapter does not set out to offer an inflexible formula for study reading. Instead its aim is to point out some methods which the reader will find of benefit if he will adapt them to his own needs and purposes.

A typical study situation arises when someone is faced with the task of reading a book in such detail that he will both understand what it is about and be able to recall the relevant details. He may be reading the book because he has to answer examination questions about it. He may be learning new facts about his own speciality or widening the scope of his knowledge by studying a different subject, or he may be studying the subject for its own sake with no intention of taking examinations. Whatever the motivation the situation is basically the same—the material has to be assimilated in detail.

It has already been argued that time spent on getting a general idea of the content, whether it is a book or a short article, is seldom if ever wasted. As a preliminary to study reading of any kind it is therefore suggested that skimming is a first necessity. But it must again be emphasised that skimming is not a vague and hopeful thumbing through but a clearly defined skill which aims to pick out from the text the main ideas and the main conclusions.

When this has been done the emphasis must immediately fall on any means which increase the possibilities of full understanding and complete recall of relevant details. For most people and in most study situations a pen and notebook are desirable, if not essential, right from the beginning. The very act of writing down in one's own words a brief general idea of the scope of the book forces the mind to *think* about the subject matter and to reorganise it in such a way that it becomes *meaningful* to the reader.

The writing of notes as an indispensable part of study reading does not consist of the mere copying down of sentences and paragraphs from the book. It consists of the *reduction* of the information to its basic essentials, *rephrasing* so that it becomes meaningful in a personal way, and *reorganising* so that it can be made to link up with the facts that the reader already knows. The stress is laid on note-taking at this stage because efficient study reading cannot be done without some hard thinking, and reducing, rephrasing and reorganising ensure that the thinking is done.

This might sound a formidable task to anyone faced with many thousands of words of compressed information. Regarded in total it is a mighty task, but if the work is broken up it is more easily seen in perspective as a series of progressive stages, each of manageable size, which will eventually result in a thorough knowledge of the subject matter.

The first of these progressive stages is the skimming of the entire work, or its sections if it can easily and meaningfully be divided up. At this stage we are looking for the theme, the scope, the line of development and the main conclusions. For the moment the details, the interesting side-lines and the examples are all irrelevant to our purpose. A brief summary of the main theme and the scope of the book should then be written down in such a way that, scanty as it is, it is nevertheless meaningful to the reader. When notes are taken the reader must realise that he is not a magpie aimlessly snatching at glittering snippets of information and hoarding them in a formless heap in his mind. The ability to take proper notes depends on the ability to investigate, to analyse and to form judgments.

When this preliminary skimming stage has been completed and the reader has a clear idea about the *general* theme of the book he can go on to the second stage which is concerned with noting down the main divisions of the book. When this has been done the reader ought to be in a position to define his purpose in reading and to formulate a series of general questions for each topic or subject dealt with and to write them down under the appropriate division headings. Whether the questions relating to a whole book can be done in one fell swoop or whether it is better to formulate questions chapter by chapter depends, of course, on the nature of the book, the reader's previous knowledge of the subject and his purpose in reading the book, to mention only some of the factors involved. What is important is that questions must be formulated. How many or how much of the book they cover depends on circumstances.

Why is there this constant emphasis on questions? The explanation is that if you are looking for something definite you will find it a lot more quickly and a lot more easily than if you are merely looking in the hope of finding something. This can be said in many different ways. "Ask and it shall be given to you." Whatever the phrasing—and similar statements can be found in almost any language—the meaning is quite plain. If you know, even to a limited extent, what you are looking for, the odds on your finding it are weighted in your favour. It is certainly true that in reading, if you are looking for something specific, you will find it much more quickly and easily than if you are "reading blind". Can one look for something without asking questions? Possibly, but usually when someone is looking for something, he will start asking questions if he is given an opportunity. If the reader can formulate questions and start looking for the answers then he is advised to do so. Knowledge is gained by asking the right questions and *finding* (not necessarily being given) the right answers.

When the student has formulated his first main questions and has written them down under the headings which correspond to the main divisions of the material, he has the correct mental set for intensive *reading*. Before this he has been skimming, thinking and summarising. After this stage he ought to be concerned with looking deliberately for the answers to his questions and formulating more questions and finding the answers as he becomes involved in the reading.

This does not mean that one question needs to be answered before the reader can begin to find the answer to another. A complexity of questions might arise at any time and when it does so the efficient reader will be able to find his way through the mist by seeing how the supporting details are related to the main ideas and the main ideas to the central theme. This is why the preliminary skimming process is so important. In order to understand and remember the reader must be concerned above all with the meaningful relationships between the various items of information.

At the end of each chapter, or at any other convenient point, it is advisable with any complicated material to reduce and rephrase the main points of the answers that have been extracted from the book. Not only does this ensure that the reader is understanding what he reads but also provides the means for revision at a later late.

If we summarise these suggestions we find that the method falls into distinct steps :

First, making a preliminary survey to find the over-all theme of the book and the main divisions of the subject matter.

Second, defining one's purpose in studying the subject or the particular aspect of the subject.

Third, formulating specific questions for each topic and writing down the questions so that they become firmly established in the mind and help to give the reader the right mental set for his work.

Fourth, reading the material, searching deliberately for

the answers, formulating more questions and thinking about the work in such a way that the relationships become increasingly meaningful.

Fifth, at convenient moments consolidating the knowledge gained by writing it down in note form using headings, sub-headings and enumeration.

It is obvious from this that there is no single skill or technique that the reader can use for study reading. The method, flexible though it must be, combines many of the skills of efficient reading, and some of the techniques used will probably vary from page to page or from chapter to chapter. The question of "rapid" reading does not arise here and speed is only of importance in the over-all economy, i.e. that it is quicker in the long run to use a method or variations of a method, such as this, than it would be, for example, to read the whole book through without making any notes. In short, efficient study reading depends not only on being practised in a whole variety of reading techniques but also in knowing when a particular technique should be used for a particular purpose.

The ability to study effectively when the subject involves a considerable amount of reading depends on practice and experiment. The practice should involve the use of the various techniques mentioned in this book and in particular the reader should make himself versatile in their use. It cannot be repeated too often that flexibility is the essential thing in study reading.

An important part of study reading is remembering. If a student has used something similar to the method outlined above and has succeeded in formulating questions, answering them, thoroughly assimilating the subject matter and making outline notes which are adequate for revision, he has gone a long way towards learning the subject matter in such a way that, given time and occasional opportunities for revision, he will always be in a position to answer any reasonable question about the contents of the book.

He has gone a long way towards this idyllic situation but he has not gone far enough. If complicated material is to be properly learned, that is, both understood and retained, the study-method outlined above requires some reinforcement.

The important point which has, up to now, been omitted is that the proper learning of any information ought to involve *using* the information. The study reader is for the most part at the receiving end of the two-way process of communication. Sooner or later he must put himself at the sending end. There are three reasons why he should do this. First, it is the most convenient method of testing whether he has properly assimilated the information. Second, any gaps in his knowledge will immediately become obvious. Third, the effort of reproducing the information learned ensures that it is more firmly established in the mind.

Two methods which many people find to be of value may be mentioned here. The first is to take chapter headings or sub-headings in the text, turn them into questions and then, using your own words, try to answer them. Careful note should be made of any uncertainties or gaps in knowledge. Then the scanning technique should be used to locate the missing information and the complete answer given before attempting a further question.

The second method is to explain the subject matter to someone else. This is valuable for students in that it gives practice for examinations and is probably the best way of finding out what one is uncertain of and what one does not know. Also, it gives plenty of practice in the necessary skills of rephrasing and reorganisation, and helps people to think logically in that it forces them to arrange the material in the order in which it can best be received by a listener or a reader.

Whatever method of reinforcement is found to be best it can safely be said that for effective learning it is necessary to *use* the knowledge gained by study-reading. It does not particularly matter how the knowledge is used—it can be used in conversation, be applied to one's daily life or just thought about, but if it is not used in some way it will become sterile and stagnant, a "load of useless lumber". New knowledge, if it is to be of use, must be given a framework and fitted into the over-all pattern of a person's previous knowledge.

Here is an example of the first stages of this study reading process. It is taken from chapter 4 of *Psychology* by Woodworth and Marquis. The chapter is called "Personality".

Leaving aside the question of motivation for the moment, let us assume that our job is to study this chapter in such a way that the content will be both understood and retained.

First, we look through the chapter to get an idea of the general lay-out and the way the writers have presented their material. A few seconds are sufficient to show that the information is presented in a familiar text-book manner containing chapter divisions, sub-headings, diagrams, and a chapter summary. The first job is to get an over-all picture of the whole chapter. In this case the work of skimming is made easy for us. We can do the work quite adequately either by reading through the main chapter divisions or by reading the summary.

If the writers had not put in these headings we should have to do the job ourselves by picking out topic sentences. This would take longer, but the actual work of extracting general information in this way would be of benefit in the long run.

Here are the main chapter divisions with their sub-headings and, in brackets, the kind of question that would come automatically into a reader's mind as he looked through them. No questions are added to the last seven headings in case the reader might like to formulate them for himself.

INTRODUCTION
(What is personality?)

DESCRIBING PERSONALITY
Personality traits
(What are personality traits?)

Distribution of personality traits
(How are personality traits distributed?)

The introversion-extraversion cluster of traits
(What is introversion?)
(What is extraversion?)
(What is a "cluster of traits"?)

JUDGING PERSONALITY
(To what extent is it possible to judge personality?)

Interviewing
(How do you interview someone if you wish to judge his personality?)

Case study
(How is case study undertaken?)

PERSONALITY TESTS AND MEASUREMENTS
(Is it possible to measure personality, and how is this done?)

Rating scales
(What are rating scales?)

Questionnaires
(How are questionnaires constructed?)

Situation tests of personality
(What are situation tests?)

Projective tests of personality
(What are projective tests?)

SELF-CONSISTENCY AND TRAIT GENERALITY
Two kinds of uniformity
Self-consistency and trait generality in respect to honesty

PERSONALITY INTEGRATION
Interaction between personality traits
Lack of integration in personality
Multiple personality

When this work has been done the student should be able to start the reading in the right frame of mind because with these questions to be answered he will have the right mental set. He will be actively looking for information and because he has formulated the questions himself he will be in a good position to remember the answers—at least, in a better position than if someone else had asked the questions. These questions will guide him in formulating other relevant questions as well as helping him to differentiate between important and less important information. During the actual reading he might pause to complete his notes or he might in some cases find it better to do them all together at the end of the chapter.

Here is the introduction to the chapter on "Personality". There are six paragraphs. We already know what the chapter contains and it is a reasonable assumption that the introduction will tell us little more than what personality is. As you read the six paragraphs try to decide what is relevant to your understanding of personality and what you can without loss set aside.

PERSONALITY

"Still keeping to our general theme of individual differences, we turn now from differences in ability to those less measurable but often very striking characteristics of the individual which fall under the head of character and personality. *Character* refers mostly to conduct that can be called right or wrong, that meets or fails to meet the accepted social standards. *Personality* refers to behaviour which, though not necessarily right or wrong, is pleasing or offensive to other people, favourable or unfavourable to the individual's standing with his fellows. The distinction is not always sharp and for our purposes may be disregarded.

If your friend, in applying for a position, has named you as one of his references, you will be asked by the appointing officer to tell what you know of the candidate's ability and experience, and also what you know of his personality. In replying you state, so far as you conscientiously can, that the candidate has a pleasing yet forceful personality, that he is energetic and persistent but cheerful and even-tempered, self-reliant, without being selfish, and that he co-operates well with other members of a group. There are literally thousands of adjectives that can be used to characterise a personality, and certainly these qualities are of immense importance in work, in the home, and in all forms of social life.

A moment's thought shows that these adjectives are properly adverbs. They tell how the individual behaves. One person behaves in a pleasing way, another in an irritating way; one acts energetically, another languidly. Personality words are not names of different activities, but names of qualities of behaviour. Any little act may 'reveal the personality' by showing the individual's characteristic style of action. Personality can be broadly defined as the *total quality of an individual's behaviour*, as it is revealed in his habits of thought and expression, his attitudes and interests, his manner of acting, and his personal philosophy of life.

Personality is potentially the most interesting part of psychology. If a psychologist is asked to 'Tell us something about your subject' he will probably ask his audience to be more specific. 'What topic would you like to have me discuss?' 'Oh, tell us about personality', is usually the answer. 'Well, what would you like to hear about personality—in case I know it myself?' The two most likely questions are: (1) How to judge personality, and (2) How to develop and improve personality. 'Tell us how to size up a new acquaintance, so as to know whether he is going to wear well. And tell us how to develop personality in ourselves.' This second question broadens out when one is responsible for other people. A parent, teacher, priest, psychiatrist, or psychological counsellor wants to know how to improve the personality of other people.

When addressing students, the psychologist is not going to hand out a set of mechanical rules for judging or improving personality. His job with students is to lead them to some basic knowledge. Just as the electrical engineer bases his practical control on scientific knowledge of electricity, so the psychological engineer must proceed from a knowledge of cause and effect.

The present chapter gives a scientific approach to the problem of judging personality, and the following chapter looks into the question of causes or sources which must be known by anyone who seeks to improve personality."

After reading the introduction we can note down the answer to our first general question, "What is personality?" Personality is: "The total quality of an individual's behaviour as it is revealed in his habits of thought and expression, his attitudes and interests, his manner of acting, and his personal philosophy of life." The student may care to rephrase this, but as it is already compressed and very carefully phrased he may as well note down the original or, depending on his purposes, even reduce it to "the total quality of an individual's behaviour". If while phrasing his question in the first place the student has paused to consider how *he* would define personality, he will remember this new definition more firmly.

What other information is given in the extract?

Paragraph 1 differentiates between personality and character but it is pointed out that the distinction between the two (i.e. the moral aspects of character) is here irrelevant.

Paragraph 2 tells us that personality is made up of a tremendous number of qualities which are of immense importance.

Paragraph 3 gives us the definition and stresses that if we think of personality we must think in terms of behaviour.

Paragraph 4 mentions the great interest which people have in studying personality.

Paragraph 5 emphasises that there are no mechanical rules about judging or improving personality but that some basic knowledge is essential.

Paragraph 6 tells us that this basic knowledge, which is largely concerned with causes or sources, will be given in the remainder of the chapter.

For the purpose of note-taking the reader who is equipped to read a book on elementary psychology would need no more than the definition of personality. If we turn to the summary at the end of the chapter we find that only the definition is given there. What then is the point of reading the entire introduction if the main information has already been extracted for us in the summary? The question is perhaps worth asking, but it is easily answered. It is necessary to read the text because there the essential information is put into a meaningful context. If the author knows his job he will also go to some trouble to make the information interesting and to find some points of connection with the reader's own experience. Material which is interesting and meaningful will be understood better and remembered longer than a bare reduced statement, even though it takes considerably less time to read the summary. Also, the fact that the reader has decided for himself what the main statements are means that he has considered and thought about the subsidiary information and consequently if he should wish to recall it he will stand a good chance of being able to do so.

Having finished the entire chapter and done the note-making, the student would do well to check his notes with any summary that has been given by the writer. When he is sure that his notes represent a fair account of the main information given he should attempt to recall these points from memory or to set himself particular questions and answer them before continuing with the next chapter.

This is what is meant by study reading. It is not rapid but it is economical. It demands hard work but it will show results. It is not rigid but can be adapted to suit personal requirements. It requires a preliminary reading of the material and the making of proper plans for its assimilation. To study successfully the reader should be efficient in the various reading skills and techniques. He needs also to know something of the psychological factors involved in reading and in learning.

A common objection to any method of study reading such as the one given here is that it may be all right for certain kinds of text-books but not for the kind of studying which involves figures, calculations and important examples of how to work things out. Some facts might be less important than others, but they can still be necessary and examples might be the crux of the whole material. With this kind of objection we always come back to the point about flexibility. The details of study methods can only be worked out when a proper preliminary reading has been made and the reader's needs and purposes clearly defined.

Here for instance is an extract from a *Sunday Times* article dealing with *The Trachtenberg Speed System of Basic*

Mathematics by Ann Cutler and Rudolph McShane (Souvenir Press Ltd.).

"The Trachtenberg system is based on procedures radically different from the conventional methods. There are no multiplication tables, no division. To learn the system you need only be able to count. The method is based on a series of keys which must be memorised. Once you have learned them, arithmetic becomes delightfully easy because you will be able to 'read' your numbers.

In the Trachtenberg system, multiplication is done without memorising tables. Instead, a number of simple rules are used which rapidly become automatic. For instance, if we are to multiply a number, say 721324 by 11, we follow these rules :

$$721324 \times 11$$

Step 1 : First write down the right-hand figure in the number. It becomes the right-hand figure in the answer :

4

Step 2 : Then, taking the next figure in the number, 2, add it to the 4 and write that in the answer, 2 plus 4 is 6 :

64

Continue working from right to left of the number, adding each figure in turn to its right-hand neighbour : 3 plus 2 is 5, 1 plus 3 is 4 and so on until you have :

934564

Step 3 : Finally, the left-hand figure of the number becomes the left-hand figure of the answer. So the final answer is :

7934564

Sometimes you will add a figure and its neighbour and get a two-figure answer : 5 plus 8 is 13. In that case write the 3 in the answer and carry the 1 in the usual way of an addition sum.

Multiply by 12

Trachtenberg worked out similar rules for all the other tables, except the 2 times table. For instance, to multiply by

12 the rule is double each figure in the number and add its
right-hand neighbour. So you can write it down :

/21324 × 12

8	2 times 4 is 8
88	2 times 2 is 4
	and 4 is 8
888	2 times 3 is 6
	and 2 is 8
5888	2 times 1 is 2
	and 3 is 5

and so on giving the answer :

8655888"

Even a cursory glance at this extract will show that the
techniques which need to be emphasised are those which
have to do with detailed learning and remembering. But it
is still necessary to define one's purpose and so we would
begin by skimming the material very rapidly. This shows
that it is part of an account of a method of learning arithmetic. The method, based on a system of keys which must
be memorised, makes arithmetic easy, and the only qualification for learning it is the ability to count.

This information is necessary before any detailed reading
begins. The reader *must* know before he starts whether or
not he is likely to benefit from the reading. If a knowledge
of higher calculus is needed instead of just the ability to
count, he would know straightaway, if he had never got
beyond long division, that the article was not for him. But
having decided that he can cope with the article his purpose
in reading it is still undefined. He might, for instance, pas-
sionately want to learn this system because he never learnt
his multiplication tables properly. Or he might want to
check through the system to find if it is foolproof. Or he
might want to look at it more casually just to see how it
works and with no desire to learn it thoroughly.

In the case of this article, whatever the reader's purpose
there is little choice of method. He is faced with a series of

rules and sooner or later, if he is going to see how the system works, he must practise applying them. Different people would set about this piece of study-reading in different ways —some might look through the examples quickly and then learn the rules off by heart and practise applying them. Probably the most effective way for most people would be to follow through the examples given, then, referring to the rules, work out a similar example and then attempt to do several more without referring to the rules. The reader determined to learn the system thoroughly would, after looking through the examples in the complete article, practise using them at odd moments or as part of his everyday work, or practise them by teaching the method to someone else.

So far as study reading is concerned it will be found that flexibility means emphasising one stage of the above method at the expense of another stage. The method to be used depends on the type of material, and so skimming and defining the purpose are necessary in all cases. But however the studying takes place, if it is to be effective it has to be practised. It is not sufficient just to follow slavishly a set method or to work one out in theory. The reader who can use a variety of reading techniques efficiently will soon be able to deal effectively with the most intensive study reading.

CHAPTER 13

Critical Reading

STUDY reading involves thinking, but for the most part this thinking is concentrated on making the information meaningful to the student. In many cases it is concerned with selected, objectively written text-books where the facts given are not in doubt. The student is mostly concerned with understanding and retaining the information. But sooner or later, depending on the kind of subject matter being read, he will find that not only does he have to *identify* information, but he also has to *evaluate* it.

It can be said, then, that study reading is primarily concerned with the identification and learning of the information, whereas critical reading is largely concerned with comparing, analysing and evaluating the information, and finally forming an opinion about the author's thoughts and presentation of facts.

In reading some kinds of books the reader must, of course, apply the techniques of study reading as well as those of critical reading, but in many cases the two processes can be regarded as separate. For instance, if we are reading an account of how an internal-combustion engine works and we know that the information is presented in a text-book that is recognised as sound, we do not need to evaluate the information provided that our purpose in reading is to find out how an internal-combustion engine works. But if the book is an attempt to convince us that one design of engine is better than another we must also be concerned with evaluation. If we are already familiar with how both engines work the reading will be almost entirely concerned with evaluation. That is basically what is meant by sub-dividing study reading and critical reading, although it must be borne in mind that both kinds of reading can and often do take place during the reading of one single paragraph.

The real purpose of critical reading is to find out whether

the details which the writer presents do in fact support the ideas that he offers and the conclusions he reaches.

Many standard text-books on technical subjects are emotionally neutral and need not be read in a critical way. But if we consider the mass of published material it becomes obvious that most of it deliberately aims at *convincing* the reader. Therefore an efficient reader must be able to query the author's thoughts in such a way that he is able to arrive at a just evaluation of the information.

The efficient reader is never mesmerised by print and suffers from no emotional naïvety about words. In particular, he is able to cope with any kind of propaganda material intended to influence the reader, and with any kind of material which is slanted towards a particular policy or which exhibits a definite tone or mood. This kind of material we can conveniently refer to as propaganda. This is not intended as a slur on any material that is referred to as propaganda. It is a misuse of the word to associate it with untruths or to assume that there must necessarily be something underhand about it. All that is being said here is that the efficient reader must be able to detect material which is deliberately organised to propagate a particular doctrine or belief, and to read it in such a way that he can form an unbiased opinion of the information given.

The kind of writing referred to as propaganda includes any material which takes a definite line on any question which needs to be argued out. It includes the leading articles of newspapers, the literature presented by political parties and the books, for example, of D. H. Lawrence and F. R. Leavis. But the use of the term implies no disrespect for these excellent writers. They would want their work to be read critically.

How do we read critically? The important thing in critical reading is the reader's *total* reaction to the ideas put forward. Any sub-divisions made here are therefore made for the purpose of clarity and not to suggest that there are particular elements of critical reading which can be isolated and used at particular moments.

In order to have an efficient total reaction the reader must learn some particular skills. Critical reading depends for its effectiveness on being able to read with a questioning mind. But that in itself is insufficient. In addition the reader must be able to think logically, to differentiate between fact and opinion, and to keep his prejudices out of the way. This is very easy to say but very difficult to learn. Perhaps the greatest help here is to study the methods used by advertisers and others. Books such as *Straight and Crooked Thinking* by R. H. Thouless and *Teach Yourself to Think* by R. W. Jepson will be found of value. Briefly it can be said that the writer whose main aim is to persuade is likely to be concerned at times with disguising opinion to make it seem like fact, putting forward disguised emotive appeals, or misleading the reader by using a variety of tricks.

A study of advertisements gives the reader something of the correct attitude for critical reading. Here are three examples of some advertising techniques which ought to be read critically if the reader is not to be unduly influenced.

"Try a Smoothie . . .

Everyone wants to be non-conformist in his attitude to life . . . wants to do something different from the other chaps. And why not? No point in always following the crowd. Of course, there are some people you can follow confidently, discriminating people . . . the kind who smoke only Smoothies. Follow their impeccable example and ask always for Smoothies. . . . Try a little of this conformity next time you're buying cigarettes—you'll find yourself in good company."

If we wish to read this critically there are several points that we need to consider. First, there are statements that need to be challenged, e.g. "Everyone wants to be non-conformist in his attitude to life." Does everyone want to be non-conformist in his attitude to life? It is doubtful, to say the least. The advertisement implies that being non-conformist is the opposite of "always following the crowd". But "following the crowd" can have a variety of definitions and so the implication is rather meaningless.

Such points are easy to pick out. A little more difficult to disentangle is the line of argument used by the writer. If we rewrite the last part of the advertisement we could express it in the form of a syllogism, i.e. a major premise followed by a minor premise followed by a conclusion on the lines of:

> All cats have four legs
> Susie is a cat
> Therefore Susie has four legs.

In this case we might write:

> Smokers of Smoothies are people of discriminating taste.
> You are safe to follow people of discriminating taste.
> Therefore you ought to smoke Smoothies.

Is that logical? Look at this diagram:

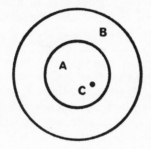

From that we can see that everything in the A circle must also be in the B circle, and if we put a point C in the A circle it must inevitably be in the B circle. If we rewrite a syllogism

> Everything contained in A must be in B
> C is in A
> Therefore C is in B

we see that the syllogism beginning with the major premise "All cats have four legs" is logical, whereas if we give the second syllogism the following symbols:

> Smokers of Smoothies .... A
> People of discriminating taste ...... B
> You C

we find that there is a fallacy in the argument.

Apart from finding logical fallacies of this kind we might also object to the premises on which the conclusion is based. For instance, what proof is there that smokers of Smoothies are in fact people of discriminating taste? Or, why does the writer assume that it is safe to follow people of discriminating taste?

Here is another advertisement. In brackets are the questions which a critical reader might ask as he reads the advertisement :

"Today the trend is towards Moonshine Beer. (*What trend?*) More and more discriminating people in Britain and overseas are choosing Moonshine Beer not just for the sake of changing but to change to a beer that's better. (*What evidence is there for this statement? What does 'A Beer that's Better' mean? Better than what?*) Try for yourself Moonshine's extra goodness which gives you so much more pleasure than any ordinary beer—mild or bitter. (*What is an ordinary beer?*) Compare the finer texture (*Finer than what?*) for better flavour, (*Better than what?*) the flavour of the best beer money can buy. Then you'll discover why Moonshine beer is really satisfying."

And yet another treated in the same way :

"Good for you.

'I frequently recommend Sherpa's Garlic Tonic (*How frequently?*) for those of my employees who are run down, depressed or over-tired, and for those who are worried about redundancy. (*Why frequently? Why not always?*) When tired and irritable after a busy and trying day in the office, I occasionally have a glass of Sherpa's Garlic Tonic myself (*Occasionally? Why not frequently if he recommends it frequently for those of his employees who are over-tired?*) and invariably find that it "does me good", (*What does this mean? And why is it in inverted commas?*) restoring strength and enthusiasm.

MANAGING DIRECTOR.

"The Managing Director who wrote this letter has kindly allowed us to publish it" (*Why? Is he a successful Managing Director? Does he need to earn money in this way?*).

This kind of advertising has a tremendous effect, but an efficient reader ought not to be influenced in any way by such writing.

Usually we do not know who the writers of the advertisements are, nor do we know much if anything about the products they are trying to sell. But by the very nature of the writing we know two things : First, that the writer is persuading us to buy what he has to offer. He may be doing this in a variety of subtle ways, directly or indirectly, but though we may not be completely sure of his methods at least we ought to be sure of his motives. Second, that in order to assess the writing properly we need to view it critically. To view anything critically means to view it with a questioning mind, that is, to formulate questions from the material presented in the way in which these three advertisements have been treated.

Asking questions such as these enables us to evaluate written material because it shows us how the persuasion takes place. A study of any group of advertisements where words are used will soon reveal what kinds of persuasive techniques are used, and will also give the reader a certain amount of inoculation against their insidious effects.

If all advertisements are designed primarily to persuade people to buy something, and most written material is presented to convince people of something or to persuade them to accept some particular line of thought, it follows that basically the same kind of persuasive techniques are going to be applied in both cases. The efficient reader must, therefore, make himself aware of the techniques.

Reliable evaluation rests on the ability to decide what is fact and what is not. As well as being able to differentiate between fact and opinion the reader must be sufficiently tolerant not to allow his own personal opinion to intrude too early. To do this effectively he must have a wide background of factual knowledge, both general and particular, and be able to think logically and pick out logical fallacies as well as assessing whether information is in accordance with relevant existing knowledge.

Most of us fall far short of perfection when it comes to critical reading, because we are human beings and therefore guided by our emotions as well as our reason. But there is no reason why we should not attain a high degree of skill as critical readers if we use our efficient reading techniques properly.

Here is an extract from Professor G. M. Carstairs' third Reith Lecture *Vicissitudes of Adolescence*. In reading this passage we are really doing three things :

First, we are *identifying* the facts and opinions which Professor Carstairs is presenting so that, after reading the passage (which we must remember is only part of a series of lectures[1]) we shall know on what his conclusions are based.

Second, we are considering *how* these facts and opinions are presented. We are considering the words he uses, the kinds of arguments, the type of evidence. We want to know what methods he is using to persuade us to agree with his opinions and conclusions.

Third, we are evaluating the passage in order to assess whether or not his general conclusions are justifiable in the light of the evidence he presents.

A good critical reader might manage this process of identification and evaluation at one reading, though he would be reading slowly because he would need to pause to think, or to check facts. In this case we shall read it three times. The first time to identify the information without colouring it with our own personal opinions. The second time to consider how the information is presented, and to formulate questions at various points in the passage. The third time to evaluate the passage. What we are ultimately interested in is our total reaction to the passage as a whole.

Here is the passage :

"If we turn to consider young people's sexual behaviour today, we encounter many vehement opinions, but little

[1] The complete text of the B.B.C. Reith Lectures for 1962 by G. M. Carstairs, *This Island Now*, is published by the Hogarth Press.

reliable information. There has been no Kinsey survey in Britain. It is frequently asserted that teenagers today are precociously active in sex relationships. On purely biological grounds, this need not surprise us because one of the consequences of improved health and nutrition has been a steady lowering of the age of puberty : a hundred years ago the mean age at which girls began to menstruate was seventeen years, now it is thirteen and a half. In keeping with this physiological change, the mean age of marriage has declined during the present century; but there is still a delay of several years between the time when young people are physically ready for sexual experience, and their becoming either emotionally mature or economically independent. Precisely at this time modern advertising, films, and popular reading expose them to constant sexual stimulation.

The increasing number of cases of venereal disease in young people, and the fact that in 1961 no less than 31 per cent. of girls who married while in their teens were pregnant at the time of their wedding, are two indications of precocious sexual behaviour in our society. And yet, what do we mean by 'precocious'? Biologically and emotionally, children are capable of enjoying sexual relationships from the age of puberty. In many societies they are positively encouraged to do so; every Trobriand Island boy and girl, every young Samoan, every young member of Indian jungle tribes like the Maria, has had many sexual experiences before their betrothal and wedding. The interesting thing is that this premarital licence has been found to be quite compatible with stable married life. I believe that we may be mistaken in our alarm—at times mounting almost to panic—over young people's sexual experimentation. Contraception is still regarded as something wicked, threatening to chastity, opening the way to unbridled licence. But is chastity the supreme moral virtue? In our religious traditions the essence of morality has sometimes appeared to consist of sexual restraint; but this was not emphasised in Christ's own teaching. For Him, the cardinal virtue was *charity*, that is, consideration of and concern for other people. It was His intemperate disciple Paul, an authoritarian character, who introduced the concept of celibacy as an essential part of Christian teaching, and centuries later it was the reformed libertine St. Augustine who placed such exaggerated emphasis upon the sinfulness of sex. It has always been those whose own sexual impulses have been precariously repressed who have raised the loudest cries of alarm over other people's immorality.

As I have said, many societies get on quite well without pre-marital chastity. It seems to me that our young people are rapidly turning our own society into one in which sexual experience, with precautions against conception, is becoming accepted as a sensible preliminary to marriage; a preliminary which makes it more likely that marriage, when it comes, will be a mutually considerate and mutually satisfying partnership."

A brief summary of the passage might read like this:

If the assertions about the precocious sexual activities of today's teenagers are true, the situation is not, for various biological reasons, surprising. It need not, however, necessarily cause alarm because other societies, e.g. the Samoans and some Indian jungle tribes, have found sexual licence before marriage to be compatible with stable married life. In our own society chastity has for a long time been regarded as the supreme moral virtue, but this emphasis on sexual restraint has come much more from St. Paul and St. Augustine than from Christ. Many societies get on quite well without pre-marital chastity, and it seems that our young people are rapidly coming to regard sexual experience, with the use of contraception, as a sensible preliminary to marriage. This preliminary is likely to make eventual marriage a mutually considerate and mutually satisfying partnership.

At this stage we should be concerned only with ensuring that the information we have recorded is a fair representation of the writer's point of view. When we have checked this and are sure that we have the writer's over-all idea in mind we must try to keep our own emotions and prejudices out of the way and consider the evidence for this main idea as objectively as possibly.

First, what means does he use to convince us? Looking at the passage as a whole, we find that, although the writer admits at the beginning that there is little reliable information to go on, he puts forward a definite, though personal, viewpoint based on unsupported statements and differing kinds of evidence—biological, sociological, anthropological and religious.

In order to evaluate this viewpoint we need to consider the text more closely and ask a number of questions. The fact that the main theme has already been summarised will be of assistance in preventing us from getting lost in the details. It will also help to make our criticism relevant to the complete passage and to avoid any degeneration into mere quibbling and cavilling.

Bearing this in mind, we can now go through the text trying to formulate questions which might assist us towards a just evaluation.

The following breakdown of this passage is not intended to represent a full critical analysis but to show the reader the kind of questioning that ought to be part of the critical reading of such a passage. Although various points are isolated here so that relevant questions can be formulated in a convenient way, the reader should always remember that he must consider these points against the background of the whole passage and not as isolated statements.

At the beginning of the passage we note the admission that little reliable information is available. Then, in the next sentence, there is the statement, "There has been no Kinsey survey in Britain." Does this mean that the writer regards the Kinsey survey as reliable information?

After this some factual evidence is presented. This in turn should be questioned. For example, when it is stated, "Precisely at this time modern advertising, films, and popular reading expose them to constant sexual stimulation", we might ask : "Are we to assume that this *exposure* to sexual stimulation necessarily means that young people are *in fact sexually stimulated* by modern advertising, films and popular reading? And, if so, is there any proof of this or is it only a widespread assertion?"

We should also note that, although we are told that 31 per cent of girls marrying in their teens in 1961 were pregnant on their wedding day, no comparative figures are given for other times. Can we then draw any conclusion from this figure?

The writer suggests that there is no reason to be unnecessarily alarmed about the situation because some societies encourage sex relationships from the age of puberty and find this to be quite compatible with stable married life. Again, the evidence must be questioned, perhaps on these lines : "Is the contrast valid? Is it really true that every youngster in these societies has had many sexual experiences before marriage? Is 'stable married life' in the South Sea Islands or the Indian jungles the same thing as stable married life in modern Britain? Also, to what extent is this problem being examined from a *male* point of view? Do we need to know more about the position of women in e.g. Samoa before accepting the validity of the contrast?"

When the theme of chastity is examined, Professor Carstairs states : "Contraception is still regarded as something wicked, threatening to chastity, etc.", but he does not say who regards it in this way. A majority of people? An influential minority? A lunatic fringe? If we are not given further information, what importance do we attach to the statement?

The question is then asked : "Is chastity the supreme moral virtue?" But why is the question asked? Who, in fact, maintains that chastity is the supreme moral virtue? Professor Carstair's argument is that chastity has been so regarded by the Christian Church, and that this is not because of the influence of Christ, for whom charity was the cardinal virtue, but because of the teachings of St. Paul and St. Augustine. We need to ask : "Does this mean that chastity is in competition with other virtues? Is sexual self-restraint not connected with charity? What happens to the line of argument if it could be shown that for most Christians charity includes chastity?"

As readers, how are we influenced by the two emotive descriptions "intemperate disciple" and "reformed libertine"? Would it be a mere quibble to point out that it was Paul and not Christ who actually said that *charity* was the supreme moral virtue? And if, on checking the available evidence about St. Augustine's life, we found at least some resemblance between his sexual behaviour and the kind of sexual conduct which Professor Carstairs thinks likely to be recognised as sensible and beneficial for young people, would we be justified in asking why he refers to St. Augustine as a libertine?

In relation to the whole of this section we might also ask : "Has the writer given sufficient emphasis to the fact that there might be a great deal of difference between considering sex sinful and disapproving of the promiscuity to which he refers?"

Apropos of his remarks about St. Augustine, the Professor states : "It has always been those whose own sexual impulses have been precariously suppressed who have raised the loudest cries of alarm over other people's immorality." The critical reader recognises this as a generalisation. Has it? Always? On what evidence is the statement based? Can we accept the statement without further evidence?

In his conclusion we read again the statement that many societies get on quite well without pre-marital chastity. What does the statement actually mean? What is the definition of "get on quite well"? We note how the writer emphasises that the conclusion is his own opinion, but we still have to know on what evidence it is based. We might be prepared, for instance, to agree that sexual experience with precautions against conception is being accepted as a preliminary to marriage, but can we also agree that this is a "sensible preliminary"? We could also ask: "Who, in fact, accepts pre-marital sexual experience as a sensible preliminary? Is it Professor Carstairs? Or 'young people'? Or 'Society'?"

Finally Professor Carstairs states that this preliminary "makes it more likely that marriage, when it comes, will be a mutually considerate and mutually satisfying partnership". If the evidence for this opinion arises out of the contrast with other societies, we need to ask if the conclusion is a logical one. Marriage in the South Sea Islands and the Indian jungles might be a mutually considerate and mutually satisfying partnership, but is an assumption being made that this is so *because* they have done away with pre-marital chastity?

These are the kinds of questions which a critical reader would ask in circumstances such as these. At the evaluation stage further thought will show that not all of them are justified and consequently they should be removed. Some of them are perhaps hypercritical. This is deliberate, and it is often found that the asking of hypercritical questions increases rather than decreases one's respect for the passage that is being evaluated.

The final stage of evaluation is omitted here so that the reader may make up his own mind. The object of this questioning process has been to demonstrate what should be done *before* the reader makes an evaluation. Professor Carstairs may be correct in his opinions or he may be wrong. What is important here is that when the reader decides one way or the other he should have good reasons for his decision.

Further material suitable for practice in critical reading is always readily available on the leader pages of newspapers and in parliamentary reports. When he does this kind of practice the reader would do well to remember that, in these days of mass-communication, critical reading is not only a public duty but also a powerful protection against exploitation, propaganda and all the forces which seek to deny the absoluteness and the integrity of the individual personality.

CHAPTER 14

Practice and Enjoyment

So FAR much of this book has been concerned with explaining the applications of various reading methods, skills and techniques to general material. Most people who wish to improve their reading ability have, however, a definite kind of reading in mind usually connected with a work situation. The scientist and technologist may be concerned with improving the efficiency with which they can read scientific and technical books, papers and articles. The business man wishes to learn how to cope with the masses of letters and memoranda which pile up on his desk. The student hopes to find effective techniques to help him through a heavy reading schedule. And so on.

In each case the same question frequently arises: "How can I best use these skills and techniques to improve the *particular* kind of specialised reading which occupies most of my time?" Reading is a very personal activity. To answer such a question fully, careful studies of the reader's abilities and the type of material concerned would have to be made, and a practice programme worked out from the results. In some cases the practice programme could be used by many people. In others, particularly where remedial work is necessary, it would be used only by a limited number.

But, provided that the person asking such a question genuinely wishes to improve his ability in a particular kind of reading and has assimilated and practised the general information given in this or a similar book, he can do a great deal to help himself without calling on specialised assistance.

Whatever the kind of material involved the reader needs to know three things: first, the particular features which are most typical of the kind of reading concerned; second, the particular techniques and skills which are generally most appropriate to the material; third, his own abilities and weaknesses. When these points have been decided it is mainly a problem of adapting skills, techniques and methods to specific needs and purposes.

Skills and techniques require practice. This need for practice has already been emphasised throughout this book and it has often been suggested that newspapers provide a regular and valuable source of practice for all the skills and techniques of efficient reading. A single edition of a "quality" newspaper provides examples of many different kinds of writing and presentation. Some parts need only to be skimmed, others require to be studied intensively. Most parts should be read critically although the degree of criticism varies a great deal. There is, however, a wide range of both quality and integrity in British newspapers, and wide differences in the variety of articles published. The comments in this chapter are mostly concerned with what are generally referred to as the "quality" press rather than with the "popular" press.

To get the best results, practice with newspapers should be deliberate and not haphazard. The entire paper should be rapidly skimmed each day to find the range and the scope of information in it. Then the reader should decide which particular parts he is going to read, set aside sufficient time to cover them adequately, select his methods of reading and go about the task in a determined manner. In selecting particular articles for practice reading it is convenient to remember that almost everything included in a newspaper comes under one of these general headings: news reports; editorials; columns; features; advertising.

Anyone who is particularly concerned with the need for *speed* in his reading must time his practice exercises, estimate his comprehension and keep a record of his progress. This can conveniently be done in this way:

Timing

Estimate the number of words in an article by *measuring* the total length of the article, count exactly the number of words in, say, a typical two inches, and thus calculate the total number of words. Then time the reading to the nearest five seconds, divide the number of words by the number of seconds, multiply by sixty and record the reading time in words per minute.

Comprehension

Relate comprehension to your purpose in reading. In some cases you may decide that you require only a general idea of the main facts, in others a considerable number of the details may need to be recalled. Test comprehension by summarising in note form the *kind of information that you set out to get* and then check the summary with the original. Grade the comprehension Good/Adequate/Fair/Poor. Keep a record of times and comprehension gradings, and remember that comparisons are meaningful only between readings of a similar kind. It is sometimes convenient to cut out some of the articles which have been timed, write on them the date, reading speed and comprehension grading, and then at intervals examine the progress made by grouping together articles of a similar nature which were read with more or less the same purpose in mind.

The range of practice obtainable from newspapers is considerable.

Scanning

can be practised by taking one specific point mentioned in a headline and finding the details which amplify this point as rapidly as possible. The practice should range from fairly short news items to full-page parliamentary reports.

Peripheral vision can be sharpened by trying to read the narrower columns in two or even one fixation a line. It is sometimes helpful to do this by drawing lines vertically down the columns to be read as suggested in chapter 6.

Skimming

is always necessary for newspaper reading. No one has time to read a morning and evening newspaper from cover to cover every day. For newspaper skimming the methods mentioned in the chapter on skimming should be adapted because these refer mostly to material where the paragraph is of the greatest importance. The paragraphs in most newspaper articles are so short that they often contain only one sentence. But, on the other hand, considerable assistance is given by the use of headlines and sub-headings.

Competent skimming of newspapers depends also on being familiar with the ways in which different kinds of articles are presented. In a news story, for instance, the first paragraph usually summarises the complete story. The emphasis is, as far as possible, on the five W's—who, where, what, when and why. The remainder of the piece elaborates these main points in order of importance so that the least important details are given at the end. Sometimes this sequence is broken up when the importance of a point conflicts with the chronological sequence of events, but the reader's attention is often directed to this by the use of different kinds of type-face. To some extent the editorials are presented in almost the opposite way, beginning with familiar information followed by opinions and comments woven into the form of a logical argument from which a conclusion is drawn at the end.

Critical Reading

Leading articles in particular provide constant and regular practice in formulating questions, checking arguments, drawing conclusions from facts and thinking rationally. Further practice can be found on the feature pages and in the correspondence columns. Controversial news items are valuable for trying to find the facts regardless of the way the material has been presented. With news items a lot of time can often be saved by being critical of sources of information. For instance, a news report which begins, "A usually well-informed source in Turkey stated that . . ." is rarely worth as much attention as one which begins, "The Foreign Secretary stated that . . .".

Information and Vocabulary

A good newspaper deals with a wide variety of topics of both general and specialised interest and consequently is a regular source for the wide range of background information that the efficient reader must have. Practice in understanding and remembering information which is *outside* one's particular specialities should not therefore be neglected by anyone who wishes to read efficiently. In addition, the more the reader concerns himself with a wide variety of interests the more he will be in a position to encounter and become familiar with new words. Newspaper cross-words are also a considerable help in improving vocabulary.

Enjoyment

Some people make a firm division between the reading which they have to do as part of their work and must, therefore, do efficiently, and the reading which they do for pleasure. Although they are prepared to practise skills and techniques in order to make their "work" reading more efficient they tend to feel that if they take up a book for relaxation then they have no wish to be bothered with preliminary skimming, formulating questions, mentally summarising the information gained or any of the other skills and techniques of the efficient reader.

Pleasure, enjoyment and relaxation are personal matters and it is hoped that no reader of this book will think that these final words are in any way intended as impertinent suggestions about how people should enjoy themselves. However, because pleasure reading is sometimes unnecessarily restricted by lack of knowledge or by prejudice of one sort or another it is perhaps worth mentioning that there is really no good reason why pleasure reading should so frequently be taken to refer only to light novels, magazines and thrillers.

Pleasure is not the opposite of difficulty. We do not say that playing tennis or golf for pleasure must mean that we have to confine ourselves to patting a ball across a net or giving up as soon as we get into a bunker. In the same way it is wrong to assume that, because some reading requires more of a mental effort than other kinds, therefore we shall get less pleasure from it.

One kind of prejudice about pleasure reading arises out of lack of knowledge and affects people who tend to confine themselves to a distinct type of book. "I know what I like" frequently means "I like what I know and I'm not going to risk wasting time finding out about something else in case I don't like it."

Another prejudice is the widespread one against classical writers and some of the world's greatest books. This often begins at school when children are forced to read certain books when they are too immature to appreciate them properly. Urging children into deep water is not generally regarded as the best way of teaching them to swim, and urging them to try books which are largely beyond their comprehension is hardly the way to encourage them to develop a life-long love of literature.

At the other extreme there are the prejudices that arise out of intellectual snobbery and make some people treat with derision any book that falls short of the highest standards. A book should be judged by what it accomplishes, not by what it fails to accomplish. We do not despise a grape because it is not a peach, or scorn the Welsh mountains because they are not the Alps or the Himalayas.

These and other prejudices and shortcomings could be examined, and suggestions made about how to overcome them. But much of what might be said can well be summed up by saying that the efficient reader is far removed from these kinds of prejudice, snobbery and lack of knowledge. He reads according to his needs and purposes and takes pleasure in doing so. He enjoys those books that give lasting satisfaction because he has learned to discriminate. To him reading is not a substitute for life but a delightful and continuous means of enriching it.

Selected Bibliography

READERS wishing for more detailed information about the various skills, techniques and methods of efficient reading will find the following selection of value:

Reading Courses (with exercises):
Reading Improvement for Adults, P. D. Leedy (McGraw-Hill).

The Art of Efficient Reading, G. D. Spache and Paul C. Berg (Macmillan).

How To Read Better and Faster, N. Lewis (Crowell).

Power and Speed in Reading, D. W. Gilbert (Prentice-Hall).

How To Read a Book, M. Adler (Simon and Schuster).

Other Works:
Learning, Remembering and Knowing, Patrick Meredith (English Universities Press).

Teach Yourself To Study, G. G. Neill Wright (English Universities Press).

The Student's Guide, John Adams (Arco).

Acknowledgements

FOR permission to use copyright passages the author and publishers wish to thank the following :

Penguin Books Ltd. for extracts from : *Minds and Machines* by W. Sluckin; *Sense and Nonsense in Psychology* by H. J. Eysenck; *The Social Psychology of Industry* by J. A. C. Brown.

The Secretariat of the World Meteorological Society for a feature article, "Weather Forecasting".

Longmans, Green and Co. Ltd. and David McKay Co. Inc. for an extract from *The Hidden Persuaders* by Vance Packard.

Methuen and Co. Ltd. and Holt, Rinehart and Winston Inc. for extracts from *Psychology* by R. S. Woodworth and D. G. Marquis.

Chatto and Windus Ltd. and the Oxford University Press Inc. (N.Y.) for an extract from *The Uses of Literacy* by Richard Hoggart.

Souvenir Press, Ltd. and the Editor of the *Sunday Times* for an extract from *The Trachenberg Speed System of Basic Mathematics* by Ann Cutler and Rudolph McShane.

The Editor of *The Guardian* for extracts from *The Guardian*.

Professor G. M. Carstairs and *The Listener* for an extract from the Third Reith Lecture, 1962.

Dr. M. J. Wells for an extract from "The Brain of the Octopus" published in Penguin Science Survey, 1961.

The Times Publishing Co. Ltd. for an extract from *The Times Educational Supplement*.

The Editor of the *Daily Telegraph* for extracts from the *Daily Telegraph*.

INDEX